MW01282454

FOLLOWING A
Sacred Path

Raising Godly Children

ELIZABETH WHITE

Ancient Faith Publishing • Chesterton, Indiana

Following a Sacred Path
Raising Godly Children

Copyright © 2013 by Elizabeth White

All Scripture quotations, unless otherwise noted, are taken from the New King James Version, © 1979, 1980, 1982 by Thomas Nelson, Inc. Used by permission.

Published by
        Ancient Faith Publishing
        (formerly Conciliar Press)
        A division of Ancient Faith Ministries
        P.O. Box 748
        Chesterton IN 46304

Printed in the United States of America

All rights reserved.

ISBN 978-1-936270-73-6

$\mathscr{T}$ABLE of CONTENTS

$\mathcal{I}$NTRODUCTION

GOD'S POEM

O God I love the way you treat me,
I love the way you love,
I hope you never
Leave me
O God from above.
I love you,
I love you
You will never know.
You are the best
So please never go.
O Heaven
Bless me Please.
O God make me better
Every second I grow.
Please do not make
Me fight back,
Make me see sunshine
And give me a hug
I love you
I love you
O God from above.

—*Katherine Bourekis, age 8, 2011*

Children are a gift from God. The home is their first and most important "sacred space." It is the parents who are entrusted to provide an
environment allowing real encounters with a living Christ.

There is a sacred journey to be taken in the home, a journey to

God and God-likeness for both child and adult, one that needs to be given a higher priority than anything else in family life. It is a path of seeking God together, of finding a deeper, more dynamic Orthodox way of approaching the spiritual formation of children, and a deepening of one's own spiritual life as well. And this path need not be new; it can be as simple as looking with new eyes at the way already addressed and modeled by the Church—and following it. Let us provide our youth with a sacred space to encounter God, a place where our loving Creator is always present.

I've borrowed the term "sacred space" from Anton Vrame, Director of the Department of Religious Education of the Greek Orthodox Archdiocese, who describes the ideal learning atmosphere, whether at church school or at home, in *The Educating Icon*:

> The place of learning needs to become a sacred place, a context where God is encountered and the center of one's being is touched, much like a church. If classrooms or any places where learning occurs are to become 'sacred places' they must be arranged in a way that welcomes God. God is already present in this space. The initiative is God's but the space itself can make the divine presence felt and welcome to its occupants. The space of catechesis should strive to be a place where God is accessible to learner and teacher and where each may reveal God to the other.[1]

If the home is to become a sacred space, the parent must aim to create an environment where God is accessible to all and where each family member may reveal God to the other—an atmosphere that might produce a child like Katherine.

---

1   Anton Vrame, PhD, *The Educating Icon* (Brookline, MA: Holy Cross Press, 1999), p. 128

Katherine was a student in my Sunday school class when she wrote "God's Poem." I believe her spontaneous outpouring of love sets a lofty goal for the parent: *Help me to help my children develop this kind of love for God and His only begotten Son, Jesus Christ. Let them hang onto this love all the days of their lives. Help me to provide a home that connects each family member to the divine. Let us all "write" love poems in our hearts.*

Young children yearn for the sacred. Their hunger for God seems unquenchable; the more it is fed, the more it increases. Sadly, many children lose this natural attraction to the divine as they grow older, as if the passionate flame within them lacked oxygen and dimmed slowly into indifference. Every parish can cite an alarming number of adults in its fold who appear indifferent to the Church. Some parishioners are never seen, even though they were brought to church regularly in their youth. Polls indicate that a high percentage of adults abandon the Faith by college age. This is alarming. We should be concerned and ask why this exodus is occurring.

While any number of factors may be involved, my personal observation is that many parents simply don't make the Church a big part of their family life, or at least not in a way that inflames a burning, undying love for God. An interior desire to serve Him is never firmly established. The distance between the Church and the adult person expands from a slight, fairly-easy-to-repair gap to a wide, nearly-impossible-to-cross chasm.

In my first book[2] I asked (with only slightly different wording): Is there a special path we can take to satisfy the hunger and keep the flame burning—a way to hold the child beyond the early years and throughout adulthood? If so, what is the sacred path we must follow?

---

2   *Walking in Wonder* (Ben Lomond: Conciliar Press, 2004)

How can we raise godly children who want nothing more than to become godly adults?

Other questions seem appropriate also. In all our efforts to teach children *about* the Faith—to give them knowledge of doctrine and Orthodox spiritual practices—have we neglected the one thing most needful? Have we failed to show them Christ's love so profoundly they won't ever *want* to leave? Have our methods focused more on instruction than formation? Instruction comes from the outside, but a godly child is formed from within.

I believe we must continue asking these questions, and that they need repeating in this book and in many more discussions ahead. We must keep searching for the best ways to help our youth desire union with our Lord Jesus Christ beyond childhood.

Ironically, Christian parents and religious educators often do no better than their unbelieving peers when it comes to religious instruction, formal or informal. Although it is commonly acknowledged that our greatest capacity for learning occurs before the age of six, and more emphasis is placed on early childhood development now than at any other time in history, we somehow act as though this principle doesn't apply to religious education.

We know more about *how* children learn than ever before. Yet, while parents feel compelled to see that their offspring get the best in academic and social resources and athletic opportunities, a notion still pervades that it is all right for the child to remain unaware and illiterate in the area of religion. It is still thought that Truth is too complex and deep for their immature minds to understand—that we must stick to watered-down stories in children's Bibles illustrated with cartoon-like figures that could never aspire to touch a child's soul. When religious instruction is given by well-meaning adults, it is usually oversimplified and cutesy for the younger children, and boring or irrelevant to the older, more skeptical and discerning students.

If we are going to keep our children in the Faith, we must communicate to their spirits with soft gentle voices, "Love God with all your heart, because He first loved you." We must construct an environment where they are enabled to receive this message and feel free to respond to it with eagerness.

I'm convinced that when so many people are abandoning the Faith, something needs fixing. And there are at least two places where changes might reverse the exodus rate: the home and the religious education programs of our parishes. *Following a Sacred Path* addresses mainly home and family practices, but I feel it's necessary to briefly mention our formal religious education schematics also.

In the early years of Orthodoxy in America, most jurisdictions adopted the Western model of religious instruction, developing Sunday school programs that took children out of the Liturgy and into textbook learning. It sounded like a good idea at the time. Certainly our youth needed to learn about the Faith, and it seemed unreasonable to ask young children to sit (or stand) through a long Liturgy.

Unfortunately, what actually happened was that our youth grew up lacking a soul-touching connection with the rich liturgical life of the Church. Religious instruction was designed primarily around textbooks filled with a myriad of facts that committees decided children should know—a practice that seldom, if ever, leads a child into a deep personal encounter with the Lord. At best, the child will know a lot about God. At worst, he won't care.

Some parents also had a tendency to feel that Sunday school

provided all the religious instruction their children needed—an impossible demand to place upon the best of classroom educators.

In my opinion, we took a wrong turn in relying on the Sunday school paradigm. This method has a number of common drawbacks (many of which apply to the way parents teach the Faith also):

- ❧ It ignores the child's unique relationship with God—a relationship that enables him to readily and intuitively respond to God's deepest truths.

- ❧ It is directed toward the intellectual acquisition of numerous miscellaneous facts that appear to the child to have little connection with one another, and that contain little depth due to the oversimplifying of stories and lessons to make them easier to understand.

- ❧ It attempts to teach rather than facilitate—in other words, to bestow something from the outside rather than to build from the inside.

- ❧ It underestimates the child's ability to grasp deep theological concepts intuitively. It does not realize that the mystery becomes knowable when presented in a way that allows her to reach the understanding on her own and at her own pace. Nor does it understand that the Holy Spirit *will* work in the child to make these mysteries plain when the child is ready, *if* the proper environment is built.

- ❧ Without meaning to, it gives the impression that the need for religious education ends when a person becomes too old for Sunday school.

- ❧ It can take the focus away from the beauty of the Liturgy and give unintentional support to the false idea that children don't have the capacity to participate in this most central communal act of the Church. Sunday school attendance becomes more important in the eyes of both parents and children than liturgical experiences.

❧ It needs to, but often does not, stress that home education can intertwine with what happens at church. It fails to involve parents in the learning process.

❧ It falls short of helping the child see the big picture, or how each facet of our Faith is connected to every other, giving us an overall view of God's cosmic plan.

❧ It often hampers true spiritual growth by holding children to a surface understanding of our Faith instead of providing them with an environment (a sacred space) that will allow real encounters with the living Lord, who is ever present in their lives on a daily basis.

❧ It fails to inspire a sense of wonder—the starting point of genuine faith.

Our goal with any kind of spiritual training is to help the child experience God—or fall in love with God. Experience is a higher form of learning than the intellectual approach; experience is what connects us most deeply to eternal truth. The sights, sounds, smells, touching and tasting of Orthodoxy, the involvement of the senses in the early years are what bond the child to the Faith, compelling a return to it again and again in adulthood. Knowledge, of course, is indispensable, but without a foundation of experience, it is meaningless to the child and will produce little more than indifference. Let us then strive to avoid hindrances to godly development and seek ways to nurture it.

Following a Sacred Path: Raising Godly Children offers advice to parents who seek guidelines for facilitating the spiritual growth of their children and who are committed to doing so within the framework of the Church. It follows the same format as my first book, *Walking in Wonder.* There is a difference in the two books, however. The focus of *Following a Sacred Path* is on motivating family involvement in the sacramental and liturgical life of the Church, rather than on the everyday experiences of *Walking in Wonder.* It also attempts to make the Bible come alive, increasing an awareness of St. John Damascene's words: "The Bible is a scented garden, delightful, beautiful. It enchants our ears with birdsong in a sweet, divine and spiritual harmony, it touches our heart, comforts us in sorrow, soothes us in a moment of anger, and fills us with eternal joy."[3]

Some of the activities described in this book are suitable for preschoolers, some for the entire family, and some are more appropriate for children eight to twelve years of age. In a family with several children of various ages, this should not present an insurmountable challenge, since family members usually enjoy doing things together whether young or old. Most activities can be adapted for any age, sometimes as simply as by having an older child read a scripture text or make a diorama of a story, or by simplifying something for the youngest. This generally happens quite naturally in family interactions without anyone thinking about it. The important thing is to provide opportunities for personal encounters with God in as natural and spontaneous a way as possible.

---

3   "On the Orthodox Faith," translation by Thomas Spidlik, *Drinking from the Hidden Fountain: A Patristic Breviary* (Kalamazoo, MI: Cistercian Publications, 1994)

Above all, aim to create a spiritual environment that intertwines with every other aspect of your family's life. Regard everything you do—eating, playing, joking, laughing, conversing about nothing in particular, praying, and worshipping together—as interdependent steps of one awesome, sacred journey. Protect the path. Learn how to proclaim Jesus in your home.

Certain guidelines will help with the activities contained in *Following a Sacred Path*. Several important principles are described in chapter two, others throughout the book. Their purpose is to pave the way for you—to make it easier for you to nurture rather than teach; to avoid holding the child to a surface knowledge of the Faith; to focus on core concepts: and, finally, to give the child time to arrive at the deep meaning of a truth by himself.

Something is happening when a child is absorbing the Faith and hearing certain truths. At first, she accepts them as fact because you have stated them. You are trusted. They are now in her head, but she has not yet completed her path. The facts must journey to her heart and mean something personal. They must demonstrate God's love. The journey must be a joyful one—not free from all sadness and difficulty, but including the joy and awareness of God's abiding presence in all circumstances.

Consider parenthood a ministry; you have been called to bring God to your child. Remember also:

> Religion should never, at any age, be regarded as a school subject, or an examination subject. It is one's whole life; a full-time job, filling every moment, day and night. The children must be sure of our Lord's love, His desire to forgive, His absolute forgiveness. They

must believe in His power to put right what is wrong. This may take a long time, because of perverse human wills and intricate situations, but He can in His wisdom see the way out. So we must pray and trust and sacrifice ourselves.[4]

---

4   Rev. Mother Isabel Eugenie, R.A., *The Child in the Church*, edited by E. M. Standing (St. Paul, MN, 1965), p. 123

$\mathcal{T}$he Child's Hunger for God

To discover the laws of the child's development would be the same thing as to discover the Spirit and Wisdom of God operating in the child. We must respect the child's objective needs as something which God Himself has commanded us to satisfy. . . .

When we recognize in the appeal of nature, the appeal of God Himself summoning us to assist the child, then we must always be ready to comply with the child's needs. Then we shall see how, in this way, we are placing ourselves at the service of God's plans and collaborating with the work of God in the child.[5]

By the time you finish this chapter, you should realize that:
- ◁ Children are born with an innate yearning for God and delight in experiences with the sacred.
- ◁ Understanding the spiritual nature of the child is the first step in raising godly children.

And you should be motivated to:
- ◁ Bring your child into the full life of the Church immediately after birth.

---

5   Maria Montessori, *The Child in the Church* (St. Paul, MN: Catechetical Guild, 1965), p. 14

THE SPIRITUAL NATURE OF THE CHILD

Raymond was a five-year-old boy in my Montessori classroom. His parents, non-churchgoers, had never attempted to provide him with any type of religious training, yet his interest in God was deep; his questions challenged me at the most unexpected times. Since our school has no religious affiliation or curriculum, I wasn't always sure how much information to give him or what to say. I chose to speak as simply and truthfully as possible and to inform his parents of his interest.

I can relate two examples of his unquenchable yearning. Once, when a teacher was telling the story of Martin Luther King, Jr., she noticed that Raymond had stopped listening and wondered where his obviously deep thoughts were taking him. At the end of her narrative Raymond patiently raised his hand.

"When Martin Luther King said that about God, what did he mean?" Out of the entire story, the boy was struck by a brief, casual quotation (not even the most significant point the teacher was attempting to make), in which King had included the word "God." Raymond focused so intently on that one phrase he never heard anything else. He had gotten lost in the realm of the divine.

On another day, Raymond was having a spontaneous conversation about the staff with one of the teachers. He was, in his childlike way, characterizing each one. One teacher was described as being particularly good at talking to parents, another good at art, and so on. When it came to his analysis of me, he said, "Mrs. White knows a lot about God." This was what stood out for him, even though my replies to his questions were admittedly quite simplistic. Raymond's mother later confessed to me that she felt overwhelmed by his continual bombardment of questions because she was unable to answer them. She gave me permission to teach him whatever he wanted to know.

Another observation illustrates how young children desire to grow closer to God. A common phenomenon occurring universally near the end of the school year is what we call the spring fever syndrome. Children who have been curious about everything all year long suddenly seem more interested in aimless wandering, provoking other children into stirring up disorder in the classroom, and seeing how much constructive activity they can avoid. They don't care to learn anything. Even their play takes on maddening characteristics. Boys and girls who have gotten along well from September to May now squabble over the most insignificant issues.

It was during such a period that I had a meeting with my kindergartners. *"What,"* I asked, ready to throw my hands up in the air, *"would you like to learn?"* After brainstorming and making a list of possibilities, the students voted. It was a landslide victory. Astonishingly, they wanted to learn about God. When I asked, "What do you want to learn about Him?" they responded at once, with no hesitation and in unison, "Everything!"

In her book *The Religious Potential of the Child,* Sofia Cavalletti describes several examples of how young children from atheistic homes in Russia are attracted to religious truth. After relating these accounts she asks, "For children who live in atheistic environments, contact with religious reality represents, quantitatively, an infinitesimal part of their lives. Why does it have such a hold on them? Why, among all the influences in their lives, do those of a religious nature—even if sporadic and limited—find a special responsiveness in them?"[6]

What is this God/child connection? Why do children yearn so obsessively for the sacred? And must this yearning spirit wither and dry up with age?

Understanding the spiritual nature of children is really quite simple in the light of Orthodox teaching. When sin entered into the world through Adam and Eve, mankind's nature was significantly changed. But there is a bliss and innocence in children that is similar to the pre-Fall condition of our first parents; there is a humble openness for communication with God. They walk with Him in unabashed and pure nakedness of soul; they trust with no pretentiousness. More importantly, they have the potential for great spiritual growth and grasp it readily when obstacles are not placed in their way. The relationship is a mystical one. They know but do not demand proof, nor can they explain how it is that they know what they know, because insufficient language skills impede a full expression of faith. But make no mistake—they understand Truth upon hearing it.

When Orthodoxy talks about fallen man, we do not refer to "total depravity" or inherited guilt. What we've inherited is a condition—an illness. Our nature has become diseased. "Man is born with the parasitic power of death within him."[7]

From the beginning, God meant human beings to become one with Him and to gradually increase in our capacity to share in His divine life. Adam and Eve were meant to be deified.[8] They were

---

6   Sofia Cavalletti, *The Religious Potential of the Child: The Description of an Experience with Children from Ages Three to Six* (Ramsey, NJ: Paulist Press, 1983), p. 32

7   J. Romanides, *The Ancestral Sin* (Ridgewood, NJ: Zephyr Publishing, 1992), p. 162

8   "Deification" does not mean that man can ever become God, but a god (with a little "g") or God-like.

created with the potential to become either immortal or mortal, through obedience or disobedience. They could choose life or death. According to the Church Fathers, the Fall was a rejection of life—their failure to realize their God-given potential to become "partakers of the divine nature" (2 Peter 1:4). Moreover, we do not believe that God expelled the first man and woman from Eden out of anger and wrath in order to punish them for their wrongdoing. He was moved, rather, by compassion and love. It was the beginning of another plan—a divine solution, a means to destroy the enemies of humanity: death, sin, corruption, and evil.

Mankind was originally created in the image of God. That image was damaged but not utterly destroyed by the Fall—hidden but not lost. Origen used the analogy of a well choked by debris to describe the post-Fall condition. Orthodoxy sees salvation as a process of removing the debris and restoring that original image through Jesus Christ. It is a healing, a restoration and transformation, not a mere legalistic cover-up for Adam's sin. Christ's death on the cross does not signify "payback" time for us.

It is precisely because we are born with a small spark of the divine image within us that we are able—in fact, *compelled* by nature—to yearn for the divine. He draws all things to Himself (John 12:32). And St. Basil wrote:

> Love toward God is not taught. For neither have we learned from another to rejoice in light and to seek after life, nor did another teach us to love those that gave birth to us or raised us. Even so, then, or indeed to a greater extent, instruction in yearning for the divine does not come from outside; but simultaneously with the fashioning of the living creature. I mean the human being: a certain

seed-like principle[9] was implanted within us that contained by nature the starting point of our appropriation of love as our own. Having received this seed, let us cultivate it with skill. And having grown, it is brought to perfection by God.

Accordingly, having received a commandment to love God, we have power to love, which placed in us a foundation simultaneously with our first fashioning. And the proof of this does not come from outside us, but anyone can perceive it by himself and in himself. . . .

What kind of yearning of the soul is so piercing and unbearable as that brought forth by God in the soul purified from all evil . . . ? Now God is the good and all things long after good, hence all things long after God.[10]

In the young child this spark of the divine image has not been further tarnished by a burdensome pile-up of personal sins. It still calls forth from within. That is why children intuitively know, without being able to explain what it is that they know or how they know it, and why the hunger for God seems unquenchable. The Divine Voice has not yet been drowned out by the world. The ability to hear and see with the heart has not been compromised by sin.

The fact that there are child saints shows that it is possible to preserve and nurture this spark if we only understood how—and would follow through on what we understand; if we would truly let the little children come to Him; if we fully made provisions for them to live in a way that will intensify their hunger for getting to know God better.

---

9   In my book *Walking in Wonder*, I called this "seed-principle" the "spiritual embryo"—a term I borrowed from Maria Montessori, an Italian woman who revolutionized early childhood education.

10   St. Basil the Great, *On the Human Condition* (Crestwood, NY: St. Vladimir's Seminary Press, 2005), pp. 112–114

Such a journey requires involvement in the life of the Church from the beginning of life.

WHO WILL SATISFY MY HUNGER?

In my parish there used to be a family with six young children under the age of nine; several were in my Sunday school class. They were amazingly well-behaved and eager to learn. After being around the family and watching their interactions, I felt I understood why.

The parents openly exhibited genuine love, affection, and respect for each child, without insincere gushing or unwarranted praise. Obedience and respect for parents come easily to the child who knows he is loved and respected. This is an absolute precursor to the ability to love and worship God.

The children spontaneously expressed love and affection for each other. It was not uncommon for the older children to shower the younger ones with kisses and hugs during the Liturgy. They were quick to help with the infant and toddler without being asked. Love and the ability to express love appeared to develop naturally and spontaneously in the family. It did so without the common stresses that often beset children and cause them to behave inappropriately.

The parents knew when they needed to be in charge. As soon as a child began to be disruptive or overstep the acceptable boundaries of behavior in the Liturgy (or anywhere else), he or she was reminded with a silent, firm look, a quiet "ssh," a gentle tap on the shoulder, or a few brief words. The parents didn't scold or act angry. They simply conveyed their message, "This is the way it is. This is not how we act in the presence of God." There was always an attitude of respect in their guidance, yet firmness too. The children knew what was expected of them and were secure in that knowledge.

Most importantly, the parents were humble and devout Orthodox Christians. When a parent is humble and loves God above all else, the children are being taught in the most impressionable fashion and are most likely to desire the ways of God themselves. All the dynamics going on in this family lead me to believe that the parents take seriously their obligation to meet the spiritual as well as the physical and emotional needs of their children.

If parents or other caregivers do not satisfy the child's hunger for God, who will? A brief Sunday school session once a week is not enough to make our Faith a way of life for anyone. There must be something more.

Meeting a child's spiritual needs is a tremendous task that might seem overwhelming and beyond a person's ability until you realize you *can't* do it alone. You *need* a Helper. There is, ideally, a synergy in operation in this great work—you and the Holy Spirit in collaboration. It is ultimately the Holy Spirit who teaches your child. You are merely the person God has entrusted to provide the environment where the Holy Spirit can work freely. This means acknowledging that children are full, participating members of the Church from the beginning. Satisfy their hunger. Involve them in the liturgical and sacramental life of the Church. Introduce them to prayer, Holy Scripture, and doctrine. But know how to do it in ways that will increase their love for God and not let it grow cold or create resentment.

> The holy life of parents instructs the souls of their children and
> so they naturally obey them and grow up with piety and without

psychological problems, and the children are pleased with their parents. The parents are gladdened by their children in this life and in life eternal, where they will once again glory in them.[11]

ACTIVITIES

1. It's All About Love: A Meditation on John 3:16 (for the entire family)

Print out a card with this verse on it: "For God so loved the world that He gave His only begotten Son, that whoever believes in Him should not perish but have everlasting life." If your children are very young, just use the first part and print it in large letters.

For added interest, put the card in a small gift box or wrap it like a present. Have the child guess what God's best gift might be. You may follow up with an informal discussion, but be led by her interest (or lack thereof). It is not necessary to discuss every scripture you read together. Read this verse every day until the child has it memorized. Point out that the priest refers to this verse in every Liturgy just before the consecration.

For a school-aged child, provide drawing paper for him to draw a picture illustrating God's love or tracing paper for him to copy the verse. Use a paper clip to keep the paper from sliding around.

Or, for a more formal family study, locate the verse in the Bible and read it. Pause for a moment to give everyone time to reflect on the words. Quietly ask, "I wonder what it means, 'God loved the world.' Do you think He could mean us? What gift did God give us? Why did God give us this gift? Who is God's Son? Can you think of a greater gift?" Point out that the priest refers to this verse in the prayer he says

---

11   Elder Paisios, from *Precious Vessels of the Holy Spirit* (Protecting Veil Press, 2003), p. 142

just before the consecration of the Holy Gifts at every Liturgy. Older
children can locate this prayer in a liturgy book or notice when it is said
during the Liturgy. You might want to end this meditation by comment-
ing that it makes you feel like thanking God for His wonderful gift, and
offering the children an opportunity to express their thanks.

2 . Prepare a Sacred Space

Set up one or two bookcases to store activities the children can handle
and repeat as they choose. Tell them, "This is a special shelf. The things
on it will help us become closer to God." You may keep the Scripture
card for John 3:16 on this shelf or on a prayer (icon) stand.

Other items might include any manipulative materials you have
made to help you tell Bible stories (for example, figures of Mary and the
Archangel Gabriel for the Annunciation; Abraham, Sarah, and the three
angels for the hospitality of Abraham; or items for the parable of the
mustard seed). You might want art supplies for illustrating stories. Many
of the materials for activities suggested in this book can go here.

If there is space, set up an icon corner in each child's room including icons of Christ, Mary, and the child's patron saint. If you like, add
a Bible, a cross, cards containing simple prayers, and a small bottle of
holy water.

3. Find Something that Reflects God's Love

Go outside and look for signs of God's love. You may photograph
things you see, collect nature items, or just look and discuss. Kids get
excited about collections. Collect shells and keep them in a basket
or box. Collect leaves or flowers in a scrapbook or photo album after
pressing them. Label what plants they're from. Collect rocks or pine-
cones. There are so many wonders that show us God's love for His
world if we only look around. Another possibility is to take a clipboard,

paper, and drawing tools to produce a picture that can be used as a creation page in a timeline of our salvation history (see pages 68–69).

4. Offer an Artoklasia

Artoklasia is a special prayer service offered in some parishes when a family or individual wishes to give thanks or to commemorate a feast day or special occasion. The family brings five loaves of bread, a small container of oil, and a small container of wine to the church. These items are blessed and then shared with the congregation in the hopes that God's blessings will be shared and multiplied.[12]

---

12 For more information and a recipe for Artoklasia bread, see: http://www.st-deme-trios.org/PDFs/artoklasia.pdf

CHAPTER TWO

$\mathcal{W}$here is the Path?

During the time of martyrdom, small children discoursed on Christ the Savior, on the folly of idol worship, on the future life, and the like; this was because their mother or father had explained these things to them in simple conversations. These truths had then become close to the heart, which began to treasure them all the way to readiness to die for them. [13]

When a man was in union with God, he found delight in divine and sacred things by the grace of God. After his fall he lost this taste and began to thirst for what is sensual. The grace of baptism has removed this, but sensuality is again ready to fill the heart. One must not allow this, one must guard the heart. [14]

By the time you finish this chapter you should realize that:

- Children are better able to retain and internalize spiritual concepts if you don't give them all the answers right away, instead letting them ponder the questions for a while.
- It is important to take time to reflect and wonder about religious truths with your children.

And you should be motivated to:

---

13   St. Theophan, *Raising Them Right* (Ben Lomond: Conciliar Press, 1993), p. 39
14   St. Theophan, *op. cit.*, p. 41

⅘ Help them to know and internalize the teachings of our
Faith by giving them the opportunity to discover important concepts on their own after gentle guidance from you.

LISTEN TO GOD WITH YOUR CHILDREN

I was discussing the origin of Holy Communion with a small group of
young children (preschool through third grade) one Sunday. I did not
read from a mere storybook but from the Bible itself. My presentation
of the account of the Last Supper included a miniature table, clothes-
pin peg dolls representing the Apostles and Jesus, a tiny wooden chalice and plate I had found at a craft store, and two candles. I used an
Upper Room backdrop my son had made for me. I read directly and
reverently from Matthew 26:17–30, pausing to move the figures at the
appropriate spots in the narrative, from when Jesus told two of His
disciples to go into the city to prepare a place for the Passover meal to
when He said, "This is My Body. This is My Blood."

Even the preschoolers were attentive. Some children worried that
all the Apostles wouldn't fit around the table. They were relieved to
discover there was enough room. Most of the students recalled hearing these words from the Liturgy, or from a reading card we have with
our altar model, so it was not altogether unfamiliar.

I added one small but profound gesture after verse 17. I set a cloth
on the miniature table and added the small chalice and paten. After
the Bible reading I commented, "Jesus was taken to the Mount of
Olives. The next day He died." Then I placed a small crucifix on the
table. Next I commented, "On the third day He rose from the dead."
I brought two candles from our model altar to this Last Supper table

and set one on each side of the table. This made a wordless connection between the Last Supper and the Eucharist.

We spent a moment of silence looking at the candles and reflecting on God's great gift of the Eucharist. The children talked about how much God must love us to give us such a wonderful gift, the gift of Himself. Some chose to go to our prayer table and say, "Thank You, Jesus." One boy went home and told his mother, "God is amazing!"

God is amazing! Yes, He is. But we could tell our children that sixty times a day and they would not realize it internally, in their spirits, unless they have continual experiences that open their eyes to spiritual realities and give them the language to build upon what they already know intuitively. We can guide their religious formation in the direction we know it should take, but we cannot determine which truths or experiences will appeal to them the most. This we have to leave to the interaction of the inner spirit of the child and the Holy Spirit. God directs them in the way they should go to become what He means for them to be.

We can facilitate an individual's sacred journey, but we cannot take it for her. Certain things are secret communions between the individual child and her God. However, we can, and must, journey with our children along the sacred path. This we do by *listening* to God with them. Meditating on spiritual truths with children has had a profound effect on me. It is not just they who explore the depths of our Faith, who learn and grow spiritually; I do also (perhaps more than they).

The props I use in telling Bible stories are not just cute visual aids; they are meant to be concrete materials that children can handle over and over again. They thus impress indelibly upon the children's minds a piece of our salvation history.

It might not be possible or practical to set aside a large area in the home for religious instruction. You might not want to buy or make a lot of materials—many of which wouldn't get used anyway if the children never develop an interest in certain ones, or lose interest in those that first commanded their attention. Your lessons can be more informal than my classroom presentations. It is more important to incorporate certain basic principles into your home life if you wish to provide an environment for spiritual formation.

First, become aware of your own smallness in this grand task. Seek humility. Expect to learn profound and wondrous matters too. Don't always be too quick to give children ready-made answers. When you are telling or reading a Bible story, or meditating on a certain point; when there are questions you have asked, or even during casual conversations, take time to reflect and wonder too. Give the Holy Spirit a chance to work in your children. Let them come to realize a truth in their own time.

It makes a lasting impression on children when they discover marvelous things on their own. How my Montessori children beam when I exclaim, "You have made a discovery!" Perhaps their discovery was simply seeing that one piece of Montessori equipment corresponds in dimensions to another, entirely separate material. But no one told them that. They just happened to figure it out themselves. Or perhaps they have mixed yellow colored water with red colored water and discovered that red and yellow combined make orange. You have set the activity up to lead to their discovery, but it is they who have observed and formed the conclusion. The principle works the same when uncovering religious truths. Ask questions that will lead; don't just tell. Let them think. Do not do all their thinking for them. Realize that the moment you give an answer is the moment thinking stops.

For example, you can tell a child about the Incarnation in a straightforward, factual way that is perfectly theologically correct. It will add to his knowledge but may have little interior effect. On the other hand, if, when presenting the story of the Annunciation, you stress that Jesus began His life on earth as a tiny person no bigger than a dot in Mary's womb, and begin to wonder how it is that He could make Himself so little just to be with us, the child may begin to grasp the scope of God's love. When you take time to meditate on this together, you are both listening to God. When you stress the action of the Holy Spirit in the Annunciation, you are adding another key concept to ponder.

Sometimes silence is the best teacher. If a child is affected profoundly by a story or religious truth, saying a single word may bring to an abrupt halt the thoughts the child is mulling around in his mind. It becomes a rude invasion of his need to formulate his own conclusions if you say anything. Adults schooled in traditional educational methods may have a particularly difficult time with this. We so desperately want to be the one to make sure they get it right; we fail to see that spiritual growth, even in a child, takes personal effort. He needs to find God by himself, just as you draw near to Him on your own. You are important and needed—to facilitate, not to drag.

Open-ended questions that lead often begin with "I wonder why" or "What do you think?" "I wonder why Jesus said, 'This is My Body, This is My Blood.' What do you think?" "What did He mean?" "How can the bread and wine be the Body and Blood of Jesus?" In the case of the Last Supper and Communion, this is a good time to discuss the term *mystery* as used in the Church. The bread and wine still look like ordinary bread and wine. We cannot really explain it with words, but we know it is true, so we say it is a mystery.

When you ask questions that require pondering, expect a first response like "I don't know," or simply silence. This is where the temptation to spell it all out will arise. Suppress the urge. A moment will come when the child will arrive at the proper understanding in her own time, in her own way. That is the moment of illumination—when the truth will stick because she has arrived at it by herself. And you have helped her do that by giving her time to reach her own conclusion. It is a wondrous moment to cherish and thank God for.

Yes, God is wondrous. Yes, the sacred path is exciting, but you have to provide a home environment where this truth unfolds in *your* heart as well as the child's. You have to be willing to put God at the center of your family's life. You have to expose your child to God. You have to grow in grace too.

HEARING THE VOICE OF THE GOOD SHEPHERD

A young mother related a touching story of how her six-year-old son's faith helped them both during a scary situation when they were hiking in a forest area. This mother admitted she had a poor sense of direction and got lost easily and frequently. As they kept walking, fully absorbed in their nature observations and straying from the trail, she became increasingly aware that she had no idea where they were or how to get back to their car.

Fearful that she would unduly frighten the child and not wanting to deal with his panic, she did not voice her concerns at first. Finally, when she decided she had to tell him, his response was unexpected.

"Don't worry, Mom, I've just learned about the Good Shepherd in the atrium [the place where his religious instruction took place]. The Good Shepherd will protect us. We can ask Him to show us the way out." The two, mother and child, knelt down on the ground. When they were finished praying, the boy stood up and pointed. "This way," he said confidently. In a short while they were back at their car.

The program the child participated in is called the Catechesis of the Good Shepherd. It is a method of religious education that incorporates Montessori principles and stresses the formation of the soul from the inside rather than the mere acquisition of facts from an outside source or teacher. The irony of this emphasis is that when you focus on formation, the child actually absorbs *more* facts in the end.

The parable of the Good Shepherd is the foundational theme of the three-to-six-year-old level in the catechesis. The higher levels of the program have their beginning there, adding to and building upon it. There is a reason the parable of the Good Shepherd is popular with the younger children. They need the assurance of feeling loved and protected. They need to be able to listen to and follow someone they can trust. The image of the Good Shepherd provides this. We can listen to His voice in confidence. He will lead us to all we need for our salvation. He, who is not an ordinary shepherd, but the *Good* Shepherd, is the image of God's universal love and care. Trust is the first step to faith.

In this parable we are reminded that Jesus wishes to initiate a covenant relationship with each of us. This is a close relationship—so close that He calls us each by name. We learn that we are protected and of infinite value to Him—of such value that He is willing to lay down His life for us.

Furthermore, one can keep finding other meanings in the parable as one matures. The lesson for the adult (which is usually overlooked) is the stern admonition and warning contained in this passage.[15]

Jesus told the parable of the Good Shepherd during the Jewish Feast of Tabernacles as a warning to beware of false teachers and prophets. His proclamation is: Only the Son of God is to be listened to. We can be secure in His love knowing that He laid down His life for us on the cross. The relationship becomes a personal one, but one in which His Voice is heard most fully and most accurately through the Church. False teachers and prophets surround us and influence us in subtle and not-so-subtle ways in today's society. Nearly every year in my own parish we have members, mostly young people, who are lured away from Orthodoxy by these false teachers. If this is happening in your parish, educate your children concerning these false teachings before they step off the right path.

At the core of the Good Shepherd parable lies the heart of the Christian message: We have now entered into a new covenant relationship with God through His Son, Jesus, our Shepherd. He loves us, guides us, offers us a means to grow in His flock, and connects us with Himself and one another. It is a part of the Incarnation mystery. It is part of the Paschal mystery. It is the Good Shepherd who unites Himself with us in Holy Communion.

We listen to the voice of the Good Shepherd through the Church. This does not mean, however, that the Bible is relegated to a secondary position. We are to immerse ourselves in God's Word. The Bible is the Book of the Church. It is the written account of God's revelation

---

15   The verses presented to 3–6-year-olds are found in John 10:10–16.

of the Word, Jesus Christ. Someone once asked me which was more important, the Church or the Bible. I replied, "I don't think you can separate the two." However, it is a fact that false teachers have mis-interpreted Scripture time and time again; it is absolutely necessary to remain faithful to the true teachings of Christ if we desire to fol-low the sacred path. So when it comes to understanding the Bible, we acknowledge the interpretations of the Church—the collective wis-dom handed down by the saints and holy Fathers.

What is the Bible then? How does it become a guidebook for our journey? Fr. Nectarios Serfes says the Bible is:

> . . . the supreme expression of God's revelation to man, and it must not be regarded as something set up over the Church, but as some-thing that lives and is understood within the Church (that is why one should not separate Holy Scripture and Holy Tradition).
>
> The Bible is the written record of our salvation history from the beginning of creation to Parousia. It is the biography of God in the world, and in a very real sense, our own biography. We can find everything we need to know about ourselves within its pages. In the Bible we receive life, we hear the voice of God speaking to us per-sonally and leading us in our sacred journey. "Great is the mystery of the word—so great that the second person of the Holy Trinity, Christ the Lord, is called 'the Word' or 'the Logos' in the Bible. . . . If you listen to (the words of the Bible), you are listening to God. If you read them, you are reading the direct words of God."[16]

The Bible is as indispensable to building an Orthodox home life as stocking the kitchen pantry with nutritious food. Don't starve your family's spiritual life by neglecting God's Word. Don't starve your

---

16   Fr. Nectarios Serfes, www.serfes.org/orthodox/scripturesinthechurch.htm

family's spiritual life by failing to immerse them in the life of the Church. Discover the richness and depth of the Scriptures as interpreted by the Church and used in Orthodox services. By immersing ourselves in the liturgical life of the Church, by prayerfully reading the Bible, and by seeking the wisdom of the saints we listen to the voice of the Good Shepherd.

Before doing the following activities, remind yourself to listen to God with your children. Ask questions that will invite reflection and pondering. Give them time to form their own conclusions. Focus on the key concepts you want the child to understand and avoid superfluous details. Remember that a very young child will absorb only one concept at a time. The wise adult begins with something the child already knows and adds one more concept to expand on that familiar database. It is a step-by-step process.

ACTIVITIES

1. **Creating Materials for Godly Play (all ages)**

    Doing imprints a lasting impression on the mind, which is why I create materials for my lessons that children can touch and handle as aids to contemplation. The hope is that they will move beyond a mere remembrance of the facts I have just spoken of to open their hearts to the deeper meanings involved. When children have something they can do or move around, they require less direct "teaching" from an adult. They become self-educators.

    Make Bible story people or saints to play with; they do not have to be elaborate. Sofia Cavalletti began teaching young children with nothing more than a Bible, and Leo Tolstoy reported the most effective religious instruction he ever gave to young people was when he read directly from the Bible. He was astonished at how eagerly they absorbed its content.

Children in today's society are accustomed to tuning out much of what they hear. They need something they can connect with, tools for godly play, so to speak. I know one mother whose child liked to play priest. She pinned a small sheet around him for a vestment and used a cardboard box turned upside down for an altar, another piece of a sheet for an altar cloth, and a small plate and goblet for a chalice and paten. The boy went about happily chanting and giving family members communion. A play censer can be made from a paper cup with three strings attached and tied together at the top.

I have seen photos of figures for Bible stories made from a Lego set. I found directions online for making people and angels from toilet paper rolls. My first figures for the parable of the Good Shepherd were some miniature toy sheep and a shepherd carrying a sheep over his shoulders that came from a Nativity set. The sheepfold was a green felt circle.

You can use what you have on hand, or children can even help make materials. I've used Sculpey clay and wooden peg people to make Bible characters. My figures are not perfect—quite the contrary; the skilled and famous artists of the world need not fear competition from me. A perfect, realistic look is not the goal. In fact, slightly abstract with minimal detail is best. Feel free to be creative.

Websites can be a good source of ideas; however, since they often change or disappear, I've only listed a few in this book. I have found information and photos showing materials other people have made by doing online searches for "orthodox children's activities" or "catechesis of the good shepherd materials." You might try "Bible activities for kids," although many of these do not help the child's understanding of a religious truth at all and are more busywork than anything else. You don't want to hinder the ability to grasp the central theme that appeals to her current developmental level by getting the child's mind sidetracked from that theme with something that is silly or useless. You will find the directions for making Sculpey clay people and objects in the activities for chapter seven. Wooden pegs suitable for painting to represent people can be purchased in craft stores or online.[17]

2. **Materials for the Good Shepherd's Sheepfold**

There are several places where you can purchase unpainted figures for the parable. These can be painted with acrylic paints. I've included a list at the back of this book of websites that were active in August 2013.

Another option is to do as I once did: Collect sheep from toy sets, a shepherd from a Nativity set, and use a piece of round felt for the pasture. For a fence, look in craft shops. Or, to make one, form a "snake" from play dough that will harden when air-dried. Before it dries, flatten slightly on the bottom and stand short Popsicle sticks into it at regular intervals.

You may also search on the internet for shepherd and sheep coloring pages or clip art to find outline images that you can print on cardstock and cut out. Look for a full-figure shepherd that is looking forward (not a profile). Add an easel tab to the back to make figures stand up (see diagram on page 39 for instructions).

3. **The Parable of the Good Shepherd (ages 3 and up)[18]**

You will need ten sheep, a shepherd, a round sheepfold with an opening for a gate, and a fence.

Read the parable directly from the Bible, although you may leave

---

17 www.caseyswood.com/

18 This activity utilizes training and the general philosophy method of the Catechesis of the Good Shepherd program. The training requires intensive study through an authorized CGS instructor and is recommended for anyone concerned about the spiritual formation of the child. More information can be found at http://www.cgsusa.org

How to Make an Easel Stand

Cut a 1 inch by 6 inches strip of poster board or cardstock.

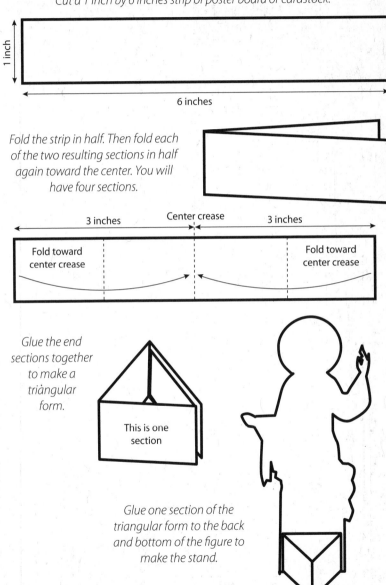

1 inch

6 inches

Fold the strip in half. Then fold each of the two resulting sections in half again toward the center. You will have four sections.

3 inches   Center crease   3 inches

Fold toward center crease   Fold toward center crease

Glue the end sections together to make a triangular form.

This is one section

Glue one section of the triangular form to the back and bottom of the figure to make the stand.

out some verses for younger children. I explain to the children beforehand that Jesus told this parable to explain who He was, and I define
the word "shepherd." I may read the Bible passage first and then reread
it using the sheep, shepherd, and sheepfold materials, or I may move
the figures along as I read. We may discuss all of the concepts contained
in this passage or only one. I may lay the shepherd at the gate to word-
lessly indicate that he gives his life for the sheep. It depends on the age,
concentration, and interest level of the child. What I always do is have
the Good Shepherd lead his sheep one by one out of the sheepfold as
he calls to each. And I always reflect on how much He must love His
sheep.

This is the part of the passage I read (you may wish to print this in
booklet form):

> He calls his own sheep by name and leads them out. And
> when he brings out his own sheep, he goes before them;
> and the sheep follow him, for they know his voice. Yet
> they will by no means follow a stranger, but will flee from
> him, for they do not know the voice of strangers. . . .
>
>   I have come that they may have life, and that they
> may have it more abundantly. I am the good shepherd.
> The good shepherd gives His life for the sheep. . . .
>
>   I am the good shepherd; and I know My sheep, and
> am known by My own. As the Father knows Me, even
> so I know the Father; and I lay down My life for the
> sheep. And other sheep I have which are not of this fold;
> them also I must bring, and they will hear My voice; and
> there will be one flock and one shepherd. (John 10:3b–5,
> 10–11, 14–16)

The missing verses (about the wolf and hired worker) can be
included at a later date or with the first presentation for older children.

When you read this story, use the figures you have collected or made, or have a family craft session to make them together.

Ask open-ended questions that will help the child reflect on the Good Shepherd's love and protection for each one of His sheep. "I wonder why Jesus calls Himself the Good Shepherd. How can the Good Shepherd know each sheep's name? Why do the sheep follow only the Good Shepherd? What could make the Good Shepherd willing to lay down His life for his sheep? I wonder if Jesus was talking about sheep like we see in the fields. Or was He talking about something else? Who are the sheep really? The sheep must be very precious to the Good Shepherd. I wonder why?"

Don't tell the children that we are the sheep. Let them discover that awesome truth themselves. I've always found it interesting that even if the younger ones have heard another child blurt out the answer, when asked, "Who are the sheep?" they still will not realize that fact until they are ready. But once they have realized it, they never forget.

The primary message you aim to instill in the heart of the youngest child is the love and protection of the Good Shepherd. As the child matures, you want him to understand that this love was so great that He gave Himself up on the cross for us, He rose from the grave in order to give us abundant life, and He wants all men to belong to His sheepfold. The teen should grasp the dangers of following false teachers and be able to relate the parable to other bits of knowledge.

4. **Finding References (fifth grade and up)**

Do an internet search or use a concordance to locate other references to shepherds in the Bible. Do any of these verses help us understand more about Jesus?

CHAPTER THREE

*C*hoose Your Destination

And if it seems evil to you to serve the LORD, choose for your-selves this day whom you will serve, whether the gods which your fathers served that were on the other side of the River, or the gods of the Amorites, in whose land you dwell. But as for me and my house, we will serve the LORD. (Joshua 24:15)

An old Cherokee told his grandson, "My son, there is a battle between two wolves inside all of us. One is Evil. It is anger, jealousy, greed, resentment, inferiority, lies, and ego. The other is Good. It is joy, peace, love, hope, humility, kindness, empathy, and truth."

The little boy thought about it and asked, "Which one wins?"

The old man replied quietly, "The one you feed."

By the time you finish this chapter you should realize that:

  ⚓   You will be a better parent if you clearly understand your primary goal in raising children: guiding them on the path of theosis to communion with God.

  ⚓   Parenting success or failure depends greatly on keeping your main purpose in focus when choosing your priorities.

And you should be motivated to:

> ⚜   Consider the priorities your family life has chosen and alter them if necessary.

KNOW WHERE YOU'RE GOING

Football players spend long hours in training—keeping themselves physically and mentally fit, practicing strategic plays, learning the rules, and listening to their coach—with one purpose clearly in mind: to win games. They know they will not succeed if they forget this goal. Stumbling haphazardly every which way around the field would only result in disorder and failure. The game would be lost. So football players choose to follow the game plan and stay focused on winning. That is their priority. Success or failure is measured by the final score.

A Christian parent sets proper goals and works diligently toward those goals. What do you consider to be the primary goal of a parent? What do you feel would measure your success or failure? What are some things you do that reflect your priorities?

As I began writing this book, I took a survey. I asked parents from various backgrounds the above questions, with some revealing results. Most Orthodox parents gave the same basic answer to the first question: "to raise our children with an unbreakable faith"; "to love and serve God"; "to raise our children for God"; "to be saints"; "to be holy"; "to be loving." I personally cherish a wording I've read from a founder of the Catechesis of the Good Shepherd—"to help the child fall in love with God." Isn't that it in the proverbial nutshell? If a child falls in love with God, all else that is important will fall into place.

People choose their priorities. Sports can be a priority. So can wealth, luxurious homes and cars, getting a good education, or robbing banks and using drugs. Our priorities determine how we act, and the decisions we make always have consequences, good, bad, or neutral.

Some priorities are good and proper but are only secondary goals that serve to lead to the ultimate, primary goal. These could be to meet our children's physical needs; to provide training for a successful career; to help them become beneficial contributors to society; even to help them enjoy life and withstand its struggles. Many of the answers I received in the survey fell into this category. Only a few reflected a total lack of understanding of the purpose of life here on earth.

The point is, have your primary goal always in the back of your mind as you interact with your children and decide on family activities. When determining your secondary goals, think about how they will fit in with your main purpose: Is what we are doing actually going to help our child to fall in love with God?

God gives us the freedom to choose how we want to live and what things we want to put first even when our choices are foolish or destructive. We can wander around an uncharted route haphazardly, without purpose. Or we can follow His plan, which is well lit with many guideposts along the way, knowing we have at our ready disposal all the help we need to reach our final destination.

I know a woman who chose her main priority a number of years ago. As a young adult she heard a priest pose this question: "If it were a crime to be a Christian, would there be enough evidence to convict you?" The woman at once realized she would be quite safe from imprisonment, for there was nothing about her lifestyle or countenance that flashed "Christian" to any vigilant eyes who might be looking for irrefutable signs of guilt.

Unsettled by this revelation, she determined she would give the world what it needed: proof that she was a follower of her Lord Jesus Christ. There would, from then on, be no doubt of her loyalties. No matter what the cost, she would be known as a Christian. She tried to do things and say things that would provide the necessary proof. She made a conscious choice upon hearing the priest's challenge to act like a Christian; it became her purpose to shine outwardly as a light to the world—just as Christ was her ever-present Light.

She never claimed that she was one hundred percent (or even ten percent) successful, and was even frequently guilty of forgetting her decision. Though it often seemed that for every step forward she took, she took two steps backward, she would, for the most part, keep her goal in mind. You have to know where you're going in order to get there.

A good role model for us is Joshua and the choice he made (Joshua 24:15). Joshua became the leader of the Israelites after the death of Moses. After they had wandered in the wilderness for forty years, he (not Moses) was the one who finally led them across the Jordan River into the land of Canaan—which God had promised them as far back as Abraham. God helped Joshua and the Israelites defeat the godless, idolatrous tribes who inhabited Canaan.

Symbolically, the Orthodox Church interprets the battles Joshua fought as battles against evil and Joshua as a type of Christ. Just as God helped Joshua defeat the enemy and lead his people into the land of milk and honey, so Christ trampled down death and leads us into His Kingdom. (The name Joshua in Hebrew means "God is salvation"; it is the equivalent of the English "Jesus.") When the Israelites began adopting the immoral ways of the conquered Amorites and worshipping their idols, Joshua issued a challenge: Serve the false gods of the Amorites or choose to serve the true God. He boldly stated his choice: "But as for me and my house, we will serve the Lord" because He is holy.

What happens when you don't choose the right priorities? Another Old Testament figure, a priest named Eli, learned the answer in a most painful way. He was a lax parent, never firm enough with his children, and they fell into sin from which they never repented. God held Eli accountable.

> In that day, I will raise up against Eli everything I spoke concerning his house. This I will begin, and I will finish it. For I announced to him that I will judge his house forever for the iniquity of his sons. For his sons reviled God, and he did not correct them in any way. I swore to the house of Eli that the iniquity of the house of Eli shall never be atoned for with incense or with sacrifice. (1 Kg. [1 Sam.] 3:12–14, OSB)

Despite God's judgment, Eli made little effort to change his sons' behavior, for we are told in verse 21 that his sons continued living as they had done. And their way was evil.

I suspect that one reason for the high rate of departure from the Church by young adults is that we have not made participation in the sacramental and liturgical life of the Church, or Orthodox life in general, a joyful experience. Other priorities have gotten in the way of regular attendance at the Liturgy. We have not taught them that our Orthodox Faith is a gift from God that we should cherish, cling to, and learn more about; they have ended up with no skills to defend it against the prevailing falsehoods in the world. They hear critics of

Orthodoxy make accusations against our Faith, and they don't know enough to defend it. Secular, social activities have greater appeal to young people who have not acquired the conviction that communion with God is the only goal that brings everlasting joy and happiness.

Our Faith is different from Western Christianity in crucial ways—but we have not taught our youth to understand how Orthodoxy is unique, often because we do not understand it ourselves. If we consider our children as gifts from God, then we must also realize that we have a responsibility to pass on to them the gift of our Faith.

True, many people who are no longer active in the Church still call themselves Orthodox. When they marry, they will get married in the Church. When they die, they will have an Orthodox funeral. But how much are they missing in the interim? How far along the sacred path would they have gotten if they had been motivated to stay on it all along?

How has your journey been to date?

Old Testament worship involved animal sacrifices as atonement for sin. Much of God's communication with His people lay in warning them against idolatrous worship. Deuteronomy 18:10 (OSB) says, "There shall not be found among you anyone who purifies his son or daughter in the fire" (in other words, you don't sacrifice your children to idols). You would not think of doing such a thing, yet that is exactly what you are doing when you overemphasize material pursuits, beauty, sports, or anything that takes them away from God.

Make time now to choose your destination. With each daily decision and activity ask, "What effect will this have on my child's eternal destiny?" I know of a group of parents in one city who successfully banded together to have youth sports games rescheduled to allow for

Sunday worship. Worship was more important to them than sports. How important is it to you?

GETTING TO THE HEART OF THE MYSTERY

Keeping in mind your goals, think about how you speak about God in the home. What does the family learn about Him from you? Of course, nothing works as well as example, but apart from good role modeling, how and what should you teach children in their formative years? I have already mentioned that many adults approach the matter in superficial ways, ways that impart facts touching on the periphery of a truth, but never get to the core of whatever concept they're attempting to teach.

I'm reminded of a statement that a non-Greek-speaking member of a reading group made. An author had avoided the word *nous* on the theory that the readers might have difficulty understanding its meaning. She said, "He can use *nous*. Once it was defined for me, I understand that it means the 'spiritual eye of the soul' and I can think *nous*."

And the truth is, children usually get the heart of things more quickly than adults. We think children cannot understand deep truths, but they can if we know what truths to offer them and how to present our offerings.

For example, when teaching about the Creation, most adults dwell on the specific acts of each of the six days. But what was created on which day is only of secondary importance. Children usually express little interest in the sequence of events at Creation; the realization that will strike at the heart and cause it to turn to God in thanksgiving is something quite different. Knowing that God made the sun on the fourth day won't inspire. However, Genesis 1:1 shows us right away what might. It proclaims an astounding mystery: God was in the beginning. He created everything that exists out of nothing in an act of love. The adult who focuses on the beauty and vastness of everything God has made and the majesty of the Creator who loves us might bring about the desire to love God in return.

How many times have I struggled to explain a concept, stumbled around with my words, felt tongue-tied and wondered at my inadequacy—only to have a child blurt out something so profound that her brief statement has cut right through all my extraneous language and shed it, layer by layer, until there was nothing left but the heart of the matter? At such moments I realize God has illumined one of His little children, and I am humbled. For example: "It's like each one of us has a part of God in us—like a piece of a puzzle. When we put ourselves together we see God" (an eight-year-old discussing the Kingdom of God).

At the heart of Orthodoxy lies our belief that Christ brought His Kingdom into the world and has given it to men by His Incarnation. This heavenly realm of God has been explained and defined in various ways, including "heaven," "not of this world, but of God," "everlasting life in union with God," "life in the Holy Spirit." We begin each Liturgy with the words "Blessed is the Kingdom."

The Gospels tell us a lot about living in the Kingdom and the nature of it, yet much remains a mystery. We know it is not limited to heaven. The Kingdom is here now—it begins in this world. "The Kingdom of God is within you" (Luke 17:21). But here we experience the eternal realm only partially. Not until the end of the ages will we fully see its power and glory, when Christ will be revealed and God will be "all in all." Here we must content ourselves with a foretaste of the eternal Kingdom of heaven. "Beloved, now we are children of God; and it has not yet been revealed what we shall be, but we know that when He is revealed, we shall be like Him, for we shall see Him as He is. And everyone who has this hope in Him purifies himself, just as He is pure" (1 John 3:2–3).

One way we can get to the heart of the mystery of the Kingdom of God with children is by presenting the parables to them in a way that leads to reflection and response, rather than merely filling them with facts. This requires hands-on materials that are more than visual aids but invite experience and repetition. Such a presentation demands stepping back at the right moment to ponder and wonder how such a thing could be and what it could mean.

I have noticed in the scope and sequence of most religious education curricula that instruction on the parables is first given to older students. This is a mistake. It is precisely the younger children (ages three and up) who most easily and eagerly jump to the heart of the mysteries revealed in the Kingdom parables. The moral parables appeal to children ages six and up when they are in their moral formation stage. Perhaps this is why Jesus said, "Whoever does not receive the kingdom of God as a little child will by no means enter it" (Mark 10:15).

One parable that is popular with young children is the parable of the mustard seed. Proclaiming this parable introduces the power of God; it leads the child to reflect on the power in something very small and to see the transformation of something so small (the mustard seed) into something big (the mustard tree). Children will begin to realize the power is not just in the mustard seed, but that God has placed it within them and every living thing.

What you want to inspire is wonder concerning the mysteries of God's Kingdom; a response of praise, love, and gratitude; and a reverence for all of life. You want to give them a foundation for godly moral formation and prepare them to understand how it was that the Church could begin with twelve ordinary men and spread throughout the whole world. In time you hope they will realize that the power of the Holy Spirit is a transforming power always available to us.

Meditating on the parable of the mustard seed is as inspiring and contains as many lessons for adults as for children, which makes it a good family meditation. Reflecting on the mustard seed is something that could take up a whole lifetime, so don't expect the child to absorb its depth in one sitting or one telling.

See the parable of the mustard seed as containing a message for the parent: You want your child's faith to grow from something small to something beyond imagining. Keep this main goal in mind daily in every choice you make. Make the words from the Liturgy, "Blessed is the Kingdom of the Father, the Son, and the Holy Spirit," come alive and mean something to your family. Get to the heart of the mystery of our Faith in all your actions and thoughts.

ACTIVITIES

1. The Parable of the Mustard Seed (all ages)[19]

The kingdom of heaven is like a mustard seed, which a man took and sowed in his field, which indeed is the least of all seeds; but when it is grown it is greater than the herbs and becomes a tree, so that the birds of the air come and nest in its branches. (Matt. 13:31–32)

---

19   This is based on a presentation from the Catechesis of the Good Shepherd.

You will need a small container of mustard seeds, the Bible or a card with this parable written on it, a candle (optional), and, if possible, a picture of a full-grown mustard tree.[20] You may also want art supplies, if the child would like to draw pictures, or supplies for making a booklet.

Talk about how Jesus used to tell stories called parables. A parable is a type of story that uses something from everyday life that is familiar to us. Parables teach us the secrets of God and His Kingdom. The Kingdom of God is important for us to know about, but it is such a big subject that we can't know everything about it with just one parable.

Light a candle and read the text from the Bible or the card.

Ask everyone to think about what God is telling us. Say something in your own words like, "To help us, I have some tiny seeds." (Show them.) "Remember Jesus told us the mustard seeds were the smallest of all the seeds. I'm going to give you a seed to hold in the palm of your hand. Look at how small it is. Now if you took that seed and planted it, it would grow into the greatest of shrubs, a tree."

Ask, "How does this happen? How can a tiny seed become a large tree? It takes something very powerful. How does that happen?" (Let the children talk about the necessity for man to plant, rain, sun, and good soil.) "All of these things help the tiny seed to grow. But is it these things that really make it grow? How does the seed know what it is supposed to do?

"Can we make it grow? Do we have that power? Who is doing this? Whose power is doing this? Could it be God's power? Have you ever thought about God's power being in small things? God transforms the tiny seed into a large tree. Jesus said the Kingdom of heaven is like that.

---

20   The mustard seeds referred to in this passage are black, and the tree was probably a variety of bush that grows 12–15 feet high in the Holy Land. I have used both the yellow mustard seeds available in grocery stores and tiny black seeds such as poppy seeds. Black mustard seeds are available in some areas.

I wonder what He meant. What do you think?" (If your children are young preschoolers, stop here and continue at another time.)

"I wonder if this power, the Kingdom of heaven, is just in the mustard seed. Or is it in anything else? Where else do you see this power? Is it all over the world? Is it everywhere? Have you ever thought of the Kingdom of heaven being in so many places?

"I wonder something else. Have you ever thought about this power being closer to us, like in babies?"

Talk about how we started out small and grew bigger. Ask, "Even when our body is finished growing, do we stop learning about God's love? We grow when we learn about God. Does that mean we have the power that is inside the mustard seed right inside us?" Give the children time to respond with their own thoughts. They may even want to say a prayer. Keep the container of mustard seeds on your sacred shelf. Invite the children to draw something.

With older children you can discuss who the sower might be, or who the birds are, or how God's power helped the Church to grow. The parable can be illustrated.

2. Watch Plants Grow and Other Outdoor Fun

Help your children plant and care for a small garden. If you don't have space for a garden, fill a large container with potting soil and seeds. When plants are full grown, remind the children that they began from tiny seeds.

Look for the tallest tree in your neighborhood. Try to discover what the seeds for that tree look like (if there are no seed pods, you might have to search the internet).

Collect as many different seeds as you can find in your yard or on a nature walk or after plants in your garden have gone to seed. Make a collage from them.

3. **Choosing a Favorite Prayer (for readers)**

   Print out several brief prayers on index cards. They can range from something as short as Alleluia for the beginning reader to longer ones for older children. Invite the child to choose a prayer to include with your morning prayers or to say privately during the day. Keep the cards in a small basket at the child's icon table.

CHAPTER FOUR

*S*tudy the Map

Again, it is like a man who builds a house and does not make any provision for the light to come in. Hence he will obviously be in darkness, since he has deliberately cut himself off from the light.[21]

Doctrines are not God; they are only a kind of a map. But that map is based on the experience of hundreds of people who really were in touch with God—experiences compared with which any thrills or pious feelings you and I are likely to get on our own are very elementary and very confused . . . if you want to get any further, you must use the map.[22]

By the time you finish this chapter you should realize that:

- God has given us directions, a plan, for following the sacred path. It is found within the Church and Sacred Scripture.
- Ignoring this plan is like stumbling blindly about in the darkness.

And you should be motivated to:

- Immerse yourself in God's plan and seek to know how you and your family fit into it as you observe the liturgical cycles of the Church.

---

21 St. Gregory of Nyssa, *From Glory to Glory* (Crestwood, NY: SVS Press, 1979), p. 113

22 C. S. Lewis, *Mere Christianity* (HarperCollins, 2001), p. 154

KNOW HOW TO GET THERE

Imagine a large, festive banquet table heavily laden with the most mouthwatering foods, set before you by a host whose gracious love is beyond measure. "Come," he says, "join me. Receive my gift. Partake of the food I offer, as much as you are able. Eat and be filled." You appreciate the invitation, but your calendar is already crowded with other important matters, so you make excuses. You do not attend.

But what if the host is a king? Do you still refuse the invitation? Or do you don your best clothing and jump at the chance to hobnob with royalty? What matters are so important that you will ignore a king?

Ignoring a king is exactly what we do when we adopt a casual attitude toward our spiritual life. We get pretty good at making excuses. "I didn't go to church today (say my prayers this morning, help that person), because . . ." I could write a litany of my standard excuses, but, for the most part, very few are ever legitimate reasons for not doing the right thing. Usually I am just turning my back on Christ's invitation to participate fully in the way of salvation He has revealed to us. I am like one of the guests who rejected the king's invitation in the parable of the wedding feast. Read this parable:

> The kingdom of heaven is like a certain king who arranged a marriage for his son, and sent out his servants to call those who were invited to the wedding; and they were not willing to come. Again, he sent out other servants, saying, "Tell those who are invited, 'See, I have prepared my dinner; my oxen and fatted cattle are killed, and all things are ready. Come to the wedding.'" But they made light of it and went their ways, one to his own farm, another to his business. And the rest seized his servants, treated them spitefully, and killed them. But when the king heard about it, he was furious. And he sent

out his armies, destroyed those murderers, and burned up their city. Then he said to his servants, "The wedding is ready, but those who were invited were not worthy. Therefore go into the highways, and as many as you find, invite to the wedding." So those servants went out into the highways and gathered together all whom they found, both bad and good. And the wedding hall was filled with guests.

But when the king came in to see the guests, he saw a man there who did not have on a wedding garment. So he said to him, "Friend, how did you come in here without a wedding garment?" And he was speechless. Then the king said to the servants, "Bind him hand and foot, take him away and cast him into outer darkness; there will be weeping and gnashing of teeth." For many are called, but few are chosen. (Matthew 22:1–14)

Who is the king? Who is his son, the bridegroom? Who are the invited guests who made excuses for not attending the wedding feast? Who are the guests who accepted the invitation? Why was one guest cast out for not wearing the wedding garment (which the king had provided)? What secrets to approaching life in Christ does this parable hold for the parent? What is the food offered here? And what does the feast have to do with the Church? Reflect for a moment or two. See what insights you can come up with.

We are all invited to enter God's Kingdom, but there are conditions. We must respond. Salvation is a gift, but we must accept and open that gift before we can partake of this eternal Feast. We must put on the wedding garment that has been offered to us. Symbolically, the wedding garment is seen as the white baptismal garment and a life of holiness—faith, repentance, purity, and love for others. This is where we need the Church. How can we grow spiritually without the Church? How can we remain attired in the wedding garment?

The Church is the house where God's light illumines us in the way to go. It provides His map for following the sacred path. Trying to raise godly children without the Church is tantamount to bringing them up in a home without windows. They might find themselves living in a place where the light is so dim that following God's path is more difficult than it need be. Without parental help, they will have to depend upon God for the spiritual food they need.

Our loving God does reveal Himself to people who have no access to Him through the home or the Church. My student Raymond was an example of this. And St. Christina was instructed by an angel despite her father's overt efforts to prevent her from learning about Christianity. Her story is just one of many. Yet even so, it is better for you as a parent to build a proper path in the home right from the start if you want to do whatever you can to help your children avoid the darkness Satan wishes them to live in. Build a home with windows. Consider it your responsibility to do everything you can to thwart Satan's agenda.

And make no mistake about it—Satan is out to snatch your kids! Look at his devious plan: saturate them with worldly influences in order to obliterate parental influence; fill their days with immoral entertainments; and make false doctrines more appealing than Christian teachings. Set tantalizing priorities before them to take their mind off God. Instill in them the idea that one doesn't need a church to follow God—that all religious organizations are manmade and not to be trusted. It's a great plan, and it's working better than the most brilliantly constructed ad from the most successful business corporation.

But God has a better plan. It is to bring us to Himself—salvation through Jesus Christ. He has given us directions, a plan for following the sacred path. This map is found within the Church and Sacred

Scriptures. Here we find the source of Light to guide us from our first tiny, faltering steps until we arrive at our final, eternal destination. "I have come as a light into the world, that whoever believes in Me should not abide in darkness" (John 12:46). "Then Jesus spoke to them again, saying, 'I am the light of the world. He who follows Me shall not walk in darkness, but have the light of life'" (John 8:12).

God is the King who has sent His Son to sacrifice His life on the cross for us. Jesus is the Bridegroom, and the Church is His Bride. The first invitation to the wedding feast of the parable was offered to the Jews of the Old Covenant. They rejected it. The guests who finally came were the people of the New Covenant, the Gentiles, the people of the Church. The Church brings us into a living experience of the mystery of salvation, into the eternal Wedding Feast.

St. Gregory of Nyssa said, "He who sees the Church, sees Christ."[23] The Orthodox home is the "little church" wherein the child will first enter into this mystery. It is up to the parent to ensure that the experience is one that fits in with God's plan. God's map is before us, in plain sight. All we need are eyes to see the route that is plainly marked—and the willingness and determination to follow it.

What does the phrase "little church" mean? How can you maintain your home as a sacred temple, especially when the reality of your daily experience often seems more like a circus act or a runaway train on its way to a horrendous collision?

In the late fourth century, St. John Chrysostom preached many homilies on family life that are just as applicable today as they were then. He was the one who first envisioned the home as a little church. Marriage, in his view, is an exalted calling. Husband and wife are to

---

23   St. Gregory of Nyssa, *op. cit.*, p. 108

help each other in their salvation quest and set godly examples for their children. He placed a great emphasis on the responsibility of the husband, who must love his wife with a sacrificial love just as Christ loved His Bride, the Church. The husband's leadership is not despotic, but one that will cause his wife and children to want to love and please him.[24] It is the same pattern shown by God in His relationship with humankind through Christ. God never compels. He invites and showers us with His blessings. When we experience His love, our natural response is to love and obey Him in return.

In St. John's vision, home life is not in one compartment, and church life in another. Instead, the two are interwoven in a beautiful fabric, sharing the goal for everyone in the family to become a partaker of the Divine Life. Visualize two intersecting circles with God in the middle where the circles intersect. This is the way the home needs to operate if you wish to raise godly children. Where those circles remain linked together, the child easily opens her heart to God.

One practical way to synthesize church and home activity is to live more fully in the liturgical cycles of the Church. A liturgical cycle is a recurring period of time in which certain observances repeat themselves in the same order and at the same intervals. These cycles are the maps of the Church, providing us with directions for finding our way in our salvation trek.

The Church observes a number of worship cycles. Many are now observed mainly in monasteries and are unfamiliar or have fallen into disuse as far as the laity is concerned. The daily cycle includes all the

---

24 See St. John Chrysostom, *On Marriage and Family Life*, translated by Catherine Roth (Crestwood, NY: SVS Press, 1986). Also, a transcript of a talk given by David C. Ford, PhD, on 9/29/2007 is available at orthodox-stl.org/little_church. html

services that recur throughout the day, every day of the year: Vespers, Compline, Nocturnes (or the Midnight Office), Matins, and the Hours. Thus, the entire day is sanctified by prayer.

No one expects the family to observe all these services, but a routine that includes morning and evening prayers is a must, as is praying before meals. The Orthodox individual traditionally has a rule of prayer, a selected set of prayers that he says every day whether he feels like praying or not. Even a child can choose a brief prayer that she likes for her personal rule.

Another liturgical cycle is the weekly cycle, in which each day of the week has a different theme. On Sunday, the Lord's Day, we commemorate Christ's resurrection. In essence, we celebrate Pascha every Sunday. Mondays are dedicated to the angels, Tuesdays to St. John the Baptist, Wednesdays to the Cross and the betrayal of Christ by Judas, Thursdays to the Apostles and St. Nicholas, Fridays to the Crucifixion, and Saturdays to all the saints and the faithful departed. These commemorations are repeated every week; but the hymns that express each theme are arranged according to an eight-week cycle of musical tones, so it takes eight weeks to go through them all.

Then there is the yearly cycle of immovable feasts and the yearly cycle of movable feasts. The cycle of fixed or immovable feasts is based on the solar year of 365 days (366 days in a leap year). The feast days in this cycle always fall on the same calendar date. These include Christ's Nativity (December 25/January 7), His presentation in the temple (February 2/15), His baptism (January 6/19), and His transfiguration (August 6/19). All the feasts of the Mother of God are on fixed dates. Several commemorations of various saints or events are usually appointed for any given day, though not all have special services.

The yearly cycle of movable feasts, or commemoration dates that can vary from year, contains unequaled liturgical richness. All the commemorations in this cycle are tied to the date of Pascha (Palm Sunday, the Ascension, Pentecost, and the weeks of and preceding Great Lent).

Visualize each of these cycles as a circle with God in the center. Each arc of the circle directs us to look inward and reflect on some spiritual need, or to remember something or someone important. At regular times we are called to repent, remember, reach out to others, or rejoice and celebrate. Whatever the commemoration, each one has something to offer that will take us one step ahead in our salvation trek—if we accept the invitation to participate.

The word "liturgical" refers to the work of the community. We are the community of God. Our work is that of common prayer. The liturgical work of the Orthodox parent is to pass on the rich liturgical heritage of the Church. Establishing a routine of morning and evening prayers builds a foundation upon which to develop the family's involvement in the Church's liturgical life. Many little things can enhance appreciation of our Faith's liturgical richness. For instance, reading or singing the troparion or kontakion of the great feast days, or putting appropriate icons or icon prints up in our icon corner on those days. We can read the designated Gospel or epistle passage. At the end of this book you will find suggestions for activities connected with the twelve great feasts of the year.

> The most effective means for the education of true taste in the heart is a church-centered life, in which all children in their upbringing must be unfailingly kept. Sympathy for everything sacred, pleasure in remaining in its midst for the sake of quietness and warmth,

separation from what is bright and attractive in worldly vanity—all cannot better be imprinted in the heart than by a church-centered life. The church building, church singing, icons—these are the first objects of fine art and power.[25]

SEEING THE BIG PICTURE

Try to imagine the Uncreated Light that was in the beginning. On the one hand, we cannot. For God's Light is too brilliant, too blinding; it is too impossible "to look upon the face of God" without perishing. If we are speaking of the essence of God, He is incomprehensible.

On the other hand, Jesus, the only begotten Son of God, became man and walked among us on this earth and called Himself the Light of the world. He made Himself accessible to us. We can know Him, the Jesus of Nazareth who allowed Thomas to touch the wound in His side—*this* we *can* imagine. The Lord God not only created us, but lives in us. Jesus comes to us by His own desire, and we can experience the Light of His love even in our sinfulness and imperfection.

This is the big picture, the overall theme of the Bible and our Faith. This is what we want our children to see. So we explore with them the awesome plan God has provided through His Son, Jesus Christ. Concept by concept, we follow a course that will make the presence of Divine Light known as a reality to be treasured. Instead of merely presenting disconnected fragments of the Truth, we want to connect the dots for them—to show how these fragments join together.

Think of it like this. When looking at a map, we mark our point of origin and our final destination (the big picture), and then determine

---

25   St. Theophan, *Raising Them Right*, p. 41

the best route to take, noting the places we pass through (the individual concepts we present) along the way. All this we can do best when we are not isolated from the Church. All this we can do best when we immerse ourselves in the Book of the Church—the Holy Bible.

The Church is where we find peace, love, and fellowship in a community of believers with whom we worship our loving and merciful God, and where our faith becomes centered on and in Christ. The Church is not a place, but a living organism through which our relationship with Christ takes root and grows, and where we can get back on the right path when we've taken a wrong turn. Christ referred to Himself as the Bridegroom of the Church. He called each believer a part of His Body. We are the kingdom of the Church, with Christ as our King. The Church makes it possible to discern and know the illuminating light of Truth that overcomes the darkness of ignorance.

When presenting truths to children, it works best to follow the same basic pattern. Keep the big picture in mind, and guide them gently to discover how one truth connects with another to reveal God's overall plan of salvation.

For example, there are recurring symbols or themes in Holy Scripture and in the liturgical cycles that children can come to understand, such as light and darkness, water, gift, love, the Kingdom of God, or the need for repentance. Each of these is experienced or expressed profoundly in our Liturgy and sacraments. One would not expect a child to understand any concept or theme all at once, but over time, with enough exposure and repeated reflection on certain topics, he will synthesize one with another to comprehend the whole.

To illustrate: From the beginning of Genesis to the closing chapter of Revelation, we find references to light and darkness. Symbolically, light is seen as spiritual illumination, purity, and even as divine grace working within us. Darkness is the gloom and despair of evil, sin, and death. Our entire Faith is about the Light overcoming the darkness, so this is what we will teach, somehow, some way.

For the youngest child, you can begin simply by discussing how we need light to see in the darkness. This is something they already understand. Add to that meditations on Isaiah's prophecy of the Light (Is. 9:1–2), the birth of Jesus, the Light of the World, and the eternal light in front of the tabernacle on the altar, which symbolizes the Light of Christ always with us. You can also talk about lighting candles, the priest's prayer before the Gospel reading, the momentary darkness at the Crucifixion, the victory over death by Christ's Resurrection, our receiving the Paschal light at our baptism, the power of the light given at Pentecost, and so on. Some ways to do this will be presented at various locations in this book.

To clarify and define what I mean by "meditate on," I am not referring to putting yourself and your children into a passive, trance-like state. Meditating with children means to informally discuss with them the concept you are trying to lead them to understand. It might include asking questions such as, "I wonder what Jesus meant by that?" "What part of the story impressed you the most?" Or, you can say something like, "God is so amazing!" "Let's just look at this candle for a moment and think about His words." "This makes me feel like saying 'Thank You, God.'"

Meditation with children is active, dynamic, and casual, not passive. It brings about responses like this one from a seven-year-old: "Jesus is like the sun, only not. He's much brighter."

The Church, and the Holy Mysteries are like a tabernacle (tent) for the children, and they should be under it without leaving it.[26]

ACTIVITIES

1. Memorize James 1:17 (all ages)

"Every good gift and every perfect gift is from above, and comes down from the Father of lights, with whom there is no variation or shadow of turning."

This verse is said in front of the icon of Jesus at the conclusion of every Liturgy. Have a family discussion about its meaning. Ask, "Why do you think we are reminded of this every Sunday?" Remember to allow the children to ponder and come up with answers on their own. This is important because the point at which you give children the answer is the point at which they stop thinking.

2. Creating a Timeline Book (ages 6 and up)

Timelines help us to see the big picture and connect the dots. They can be as simple or as heavily detailed as you wish. The instructions below are for a simple one that makes no effort to arrange by decades or centuries. It is not according to scale; it merely divides the time periods into *Before Christ, Time of Christ, Today,* and *To Come* categories. This is an ongoing project and is not intended to be completed in one or two sessions.

You will need a three-ring binder, copy paper, and a three-hole punch. You might also want dividers with tabs.

---

26   St. Theophan, *op. cit.*, p. 30

Each page of the timeline will fit into one of these categories, so first you need to make pages with labels at the top in a fairly large font: some for *The Old Testament*, some for *The New Testament*, some for *Today*, and one or two for *To Come*. A few spaces down from this title, make a line. On this line, after you have read or discussed a story, the child will write the name and date of the specific event.

Leave a large space for drawing illustrations or pasting pictures or paper icons. Near the bottom of the page, draw four or five widely spaced lines for the child's comments. As an example: The title for the first page could be "God Made Everything." You and your child could fill the space with pictures (glued or drawn) of plants, animals, and people. You might encourage the child to copy Genesis 1:1 or write a prayer of thanksgiving on the lines. On a page under *Today*, you could have a picture of a church and photos of your family. Under *To Come*, paste an icon of Christ enthroned or a drawing of the child's idea of what heaven might look like.

3. Twelve Great Feasts Display

Do you have a hallway where you can display some drawings or icon prints of the Twelve Great Feasts (at least 5 by 7 inches in size)? Hang them there like a hall of fame. If you have room, place them in a circle with an icon of Pascha in the center. See the end of this book for activities for each of the feasts.

CHAPTER FIVE

$\mathscr{P}$utting on Christ

*Or do you not know that as many of us as were baptized into Christ
Jesus were baptized into His death? Therefore we were buried with
Him through baptism into death, that just as Christ was raised from
the dead by the glory of the Father, even so we should walk in newness of life. For if we have been united together in the likeness of His
death, certainly we also shall be in the likeness of His resurrection
(Romans 6:3–5).*

*Baptism is not a magical act adding some supernatural powers to our
natural faculties. It is the beginning of life eternal itself, which unites
us here in "this world" with the "world to come," makes us even now
in this life partakers of God's Kingdom.*[27]

By the time you finish this chapter you should realize that:

- ⊗ Baptism is more than a mere symbol of our spiritual
  rebirth; it is the actual shedding of our old sinful nature
  and the re-creation of a new nature in Christ. It is our
  entrance into the kingdom of God.
- ⊗ In baptism we mystically participate in the death, burial,
  and resurrection of Christ; it is our personal Pascha.

---

27 Fr. Alexander Schmemann, *Of Water and the Spirit* (Yonkers, NY: SVS Press, 1974), p. 42

And you should be motivated to:

✍ Bring your children to an understanding of what their baptism means to them personally: it was the greatest day in their life, the day Jesus shared His light with them.

TAKE THE PROPER CLOTHING

A mom wrote on our parish's Facebook page, "I think Mrs. White's lesson on baptism made a big impression on Luca. I found him baptizing a doll in the sink." (She didn't mention whether the doll was waterproof or not.)

I've heard similar stories before. Kids like to do baptisms. The interesting thing is, I didn't use a doll for the presentation that Luca participated in. I have used one in the past, but this time I dipped my fist three times in our stainless steel baptismal font (aka salad bowl).

Why my fist instead of a doll? The first time I tried using my fist I understood the reason. I had an immediate sense of this action being personal. It was I whose life had once been made new in the sanctified water of baptism—not someone else, not a doll—but I myself. If that was *my* interior experience, then it probably impresses the child that same way.

Do you truly comprehend the wonder of baptism, the vastness of God's love for the whole of humankind, for you individually? Over and over again, He reveals it—we see this love in the rite of baptism. Consider Fr. Schmemann's reflection on these words from the baptismal prayers.

For him who is now come unto Holy Baptism and for his salvation. . . . The world, the Church, and now this one man and his salvation!

Different is this from human ideologies which while glorifying and exalting man, in fact subordinate him "to the world," reduce him to collective, impersonal and abstract "humanity," the Gospel is always aimed at the *person*. It is as if the whole world were created for each man and the salvation of each man were, in the eyes of God, more precious than the whole world.[28]

What can explain God's gift of grace to us in the mystery of baptism except love? How is it that He should want each of us to belong to the Body of Christ, the Church? In my opinion, if someone wants to understand Orthodox theology, they should study our baptismal rite, including in this study an examination of all the events that foreshadowed baptism in the Old Testament and all the New Testament references to this holy sacrament. For herein lies the content of God's entire plan of salvation with no missing details, especially if you consider the rite as practiced in earlier centuries, when both the corporate and individual aspects of it were plainer to see.

Today baptisms are usually private affairs for individual families and friends. Other than to acknowledge the rite as an initiation into church membership, little thought is given to the mystery—the mystical depth of its meaning. It has not always been so. Once catechumens spent up to three years preparing for their baptism, which would then be conducted on a Holy Saturday; it was a community celebration connected with illumination and the receiving of the Paschal light. The entire community prayed and fasted with the catechumens, and after the baptism everyone would worship together. The newly baptized would be led into the church for full participation in the Paschal liturgy and to receive communion for the first time.

---

28   Schmemann, *op. cit.*, pp. 42, 43

Something actually and mystically happens in baptism. It is more than a mere sign of our spiritual rebirth. It *is* our rebirth. When we go down into the water, we die to our old sinful nature—we are cleansed and purified. When we come up out of the water, we are resurrected to a new life in and with Christ. We are truly a new creature. We have personally received the Paschal light. The grace of baptism has lifted us from an ordinary state to that of partakers of God's Kingdom.

Why then is there a growing number of young Orthodox parents who do not see the importance of baptizing their babies? Many Christian groups believe that only believing adults should be baptized. In the Orthodox mind, that makes baptism more an act of man than an act of God.[29]

PRESENTING THE SYMBOLS OF BAPTISM

Children can be brought to an understanding of baptism if you concentrate on presenting certain baptismal symbols first, rather than going through the liturgical ceremony step by step from beginning to end. I begin with the candle, even though it actually belongs to the chrismation part of the ceremony. This is because we have already had presentations on the symbol of light. The children understand that Jesus is the Light, and I want to make the connection from something they already know to a new insight.

I stress that the day of the child's baptism was when Jesus gave him the gift of His light. (If the children have already learned about

---

29 For a more comprehensive explanation of why we baptize infants, read the booklet "Infant Baptism: What the Church Believes," published by Ancient Faith Publishing.

Pascha, they will easily make the connection.) Water is another major symbol; others that children respond to are the white garment, the oil of gladness, the procession around the altar three times, chrismation, the sign of the cross, and the triple immersion. We also learn and reflect on the words of the baptismal hymn, "For as many of you as have been baptized into Christ have put on Christ" (Galatians 3:27). With older children, I would also explain the exorcism at the beginning of the rite of baptism.

The white garment, in which the newly baptized is clothed, is connected to light when it is shown to children. "White is the color of the purest light." The white garment symbolizes the purity and righteousness Christians are called to strive for in this life. However, Fr. Schmemann has said our understanding is incomplete if we leave it at that.

> What it reveals and therefore communicates is the radical *newness* of that purity and righteousness, of that *new* spiritual life for which the neophyte was *regenerated* in the baptismal *immersion* and which will now be bestowed upon him through the seal of the gift of the Holy Spirit.[30]

Baptism is a rich source of abundant life within us. We do a great disservice to our children if we do not help them become aware, as soon as possible, of this great gift. Symbols provide a way of piercing into the depths of spiritual realities that we cannot grasp by means of our senses alone. They speak a language dynamic in impact. And children will understand the language of symbols if we help them because

---

30   Schmemann, *op. cit.*, p. 72

they have the ability to go beyond what can be seen and touched. When the child is young, pointing out the meaning of any symbol requires movement (physical interaction such as holding a candle), repetition (coming back to that point again and again), using as few words as possible, and allowing time for discussion and reflection (pondering the mysteries of God).

For children who cannot write, and even for those who can, drawing a picture can help them internalize the concept they have just discovered. Artwork can also provide a means to express innermost feelings and thoughts. Keep art supplies available for this purpose. Some children might enjoy copying the baptismal hymn with a calligraphy pen on nice paper and framing it.

> The Kingdom of Heaven belongs to the baptized person already by virtue of his baptism. He is taken away from the dominion of Satan, who now loses authority over him and the power to work arbitrarily in him. By entrance into the Church—the house of refuge—Satan is denied access to the newly baptized one. He finds himself here as in a safe enclosure.
>
> All these things are spiritually outward privileges and gifts. But what happens inwardly? The healing of the affliction and injury of sin. The power of grace penetrates within and restores here the Divine relationship of the powers and parts, as well as changing the chief orientation from oneself to God—to pleasing God and increasing one's good deeds.
>
> Therefore, baptism is a rebirth or a new birth which puts a man in a renewed condition.[31]

---

31   St. Theophan, *op. cit.*, pp. 20–21

ACTIVITIES

These activities are adapted from the Catechesis of the Good Shepherd. I've tried to make them something you can do at home. As home activities they can be presented more casually than at church school.

Don't try to do them all at once. Introduce the candle first (even though it and the white garment actually belong to the chrismation rite following the baptism); otherwise the order can be changed as you wish. Notice that I have not included instructions for presenting several of the symbols I have mentioned above. These are certainly important and can be discussed and/or acted out after you have completed the following activities. Keep all necessary supplies on the shelves you have already prepared. Older children may, of course, study the actual baptismal rite.

1. **The Candle (ages 3 and up—after the Paschal candle has been presented)**

   You will need a large candle to represent the Paschal candle and a small candle for each person participating. Light the Paschal candle and explain that this represents the Risen Christ. Have each person, one at a time, light his or her candle from the Paschal candle.

   Discuss each person's baptismal day—the day when the light of the risen Christ came to each one. Pause to reflect on why this was such a great day, and why the life of the Risen Lord that He brings to us is such a great gift. Dwell on the fact that the light shining from the candle in our hands is the same as the light of the Paschal candle. Help the child to discover that the very Light of Christ is in each one of us.

2. **The White Garment**

   Show a white baptismal gown or suit, preferably the child's own. (You could show a picture of one, but it will not be as effective.) Keep this out on your "sacred shelf" where they can look at it. Talk about why we are clothed in white after our baptism. "White is the color of the purest light, and baptism fills us with the light of Christ. We could say we are dressed in the light of Christ. It is inside of us and outside of us." With older children, you could get into a deeper discussion of the meaning of purity.

3. **The Water and the Triple Immersion**
    You will need a bowl of water and a white towel, plus the candle and white garment from the previous presentations.

    Review the symbols of light and the white garment. The light of Jesus is the light we received at our baptism. The white garment shows that we are a new person. Talk about the gift of water and how water helps new things grow and how we wash things to make them clean. You can explain that the priest first sanctifies the water by making the sign of the cross over it before the person is baptized. This changes the water. It is no longer ordinary water. It is now sanctified, and the power of the Holy Spirit can work through the water.

    Then dip your fist slowly into the water three times, repeating the words of the rite as you do so. "I baptize you in the name of the Father, the Son, and the Holy Spirit. Amen."

4. **The Baptismal Hymn (from Galatians 3:27)**
    Memorize and sing the baptismal hymn as it is sung in your parish: "As many of you as were baptized into Christ have put on Christ. Alleluia!"

CHAPTER SIX

*F*uel Up

*I am the true vine, and My Father is the vinedresser. Every branch
in Me that does not bear fruit He takes away; and every branch
that bears fruit He prunes, that it may bear more fruit. You are
already clean because of the Word I have spoken to you. Abide in
Me, and I in you. As the branch cannot bear fruit of itself, unless it
abides in the vine, neither can you, unless you abide in Me.*

*I am the vine, you are the branches. He who abides in Me,
and I in him, bears much fruit; for without Me you can do nothing.
If anyone does not abide in Me, he is cast out as a branch and is
withered. (John 15:1–6)*

By the time you finish this chapter you should realize that:

- In the vineyard of the Church, Christ is the vine; we are
  the branches. Our union with Him is intimate and real.
- In Holy Communion we receive God's greatest gift—the
  gift of Himself. Receiving this gift fills us with divine
  grace.

And you should be motivated to:

- Nurture your child's desire to participate in the Liturgy
  and receive the Body and Blood of Jesus frequently.

ABIDE IN CHRIST: THE TRUE VINE

My great-grandfather died before I was born, yet I've heard so many stories about him that I feel I know him intimately. I think he played a significant role in the shaping of my character; he helped make me who I am today. Was he a saint? Judging from the colorful language he is said to have freely used, probably not. I don't know anything about his prayer habits or his church attendance, or if he spent much time reading the Bible. I do know that my mother told me someone once said of him, "He didn't preach Christianity, he lived it."

Judging by his deeds and reputation, I suspect he walked more closely in the ways of the Lord than I generally do, whatever his church attendance. Great-grandfather, L.C., as he was called, cared about other people. He was the postmaster of the small town that bears his name in Washington State. At one time he tried to start a grocery store in one section of the postal building, but he lost money because he kept giving away food to those who were going through hard times.

Another time, some schoolchildren had not arrived home on schedule during a vicious snowstorm. They had a several-mile horseback ride to and from school. Since L.C.'s home was closer to the school than their own, their father came by to inquire about them, thinking they might have taken refuge there. My great-grandfather immediately saddled up his horse to help search for them. He said he couldn't rest until he knew they were safe. It turned out that the resourceful children had gotten off their horses, nestled against a hill, used the horses as shelter on one side and the hill on the other, and were waiting for help, cold but otherwise fine.

I thought about L.C. Malott when reading the parable of the True Vine. That may seem like a curious connection, but my thought processes went something like this: He is a branch of my family tree—a source of my life. I am a branch also, extending from him. We are bonded together in life and death in a very real relationship, and the fact that I cannot see him with my physical eyes does not lessen that relationship.

Jesus described the relationship He wishes to have with us as members of His Church family. God the Father is the vinedresser. The Son, Christ, is the Vine, our life source. We are the branches who need Him to survive. That is a very real and intimate relationship.

Vines in a vineyard are domesticated plants. Workers in the vineyard do not allow the vines to spread out wildly; they arrange them on trellises just so. The grapes hang down, exposed to the air, which will help them grow until they are ready for harvest. The vines hold fast to these trellises.

Undomesticated vines that grow wild outside the vineyard become entangled and indistinguishable from one another. If you were to walk in an area where vines grow wild, you might trip over them. They would be a hindrance to your path. The fruit from a wild vine that does not get sufficient air or life-giving sustenance will be less than ideal; perhaps it won't even survive.

In the imagery of the True Vine, Christ was contrasting Himself to a disobedient and unfruitful Israel. He was speaking specifically to the Apostles, telling them what they needed to do in order to spread the Gospel. This is also a personal message: We must abide in Christ and His Church in order to bear fruit as Christians. Without divine grace we will not achieve our calling; we will become entangled in a life that hinders our path to God. Abiding in Christ is the only way to untangle ourselves and become vitalized, able to bear the fruit of good works and fulfill our purpose in His Kingdom.

What does "abiding in Christ" mean? A dictionary-style definition might read, "to remain, rest, stay, wait, and continue." It means living, or walking, moment by moment drawing upon the strength, the guidance, and the love of the Savior, being led by the Holy Spirit—not faltering—remaining steadfast. Abiding in Christ is patient, expectant, neither slothful nor anxiously striving beyond our capabilities. It is inner peace. Abiding in Christ is walking as Christ walked: "He who says he abides in Him ought himself also to walk just as He walked" (1 John 2:6).[32]

How can a child learn to abide in Christ if her caregivers neglect their own spiritual lives? Or if she has never been taught how the Savior walked when He came to earth—if she has never heard Bible stories, or the inspiring lives of the saints, either in church or at home? Read to your children frequently from a Bible storybook or directly from the Bible. If you have a globe, point out Israel to show where Jesus lived. Discuss the Gospel readings. Relate them to how we can abide in Christ. Read about the saints. How can a child learn to abide in Christ if he seldom receives communion? Grant them the gift of frequent communion.

Children whose families are actively *and* joyfully involved in the sacramental and liturgical life of the Church develop quite naturally a desire to have this unique relationship with the Lord. It happens almost without anyone being aware of it, seemingly without extraordinary effort. If you wait until they are "old enough to understand what

---

32   See also Matt. 7:19–20; Gal. 5:22–23; 1 John 2:15–17, 24; James 5:7

is happening" or until they learn how to behave well enough so they don't embarrass you, that will be too late. Any effort you make will likely be taxing and insufficient. It might very well meet with rebellion.

UNDERSTANDING THE HEART OF THE LITURGY

The way children learn to understand the Liturgy is by being there (albeit they will need a little guidance from you). The way children learn to behave properly in church is by being there (of course, also with some guidance). Yes, children may get bored and restless. They may sometimes make not-so-joyful noises unto the Lord. They may embarrass and frustrate you. You may feel as if concentrating on your own worship is a lost cause, that it might be easier to hold off on church attendance for a while.

If you believe your children can't handle being in church for an hour and a half, you've probably dealt with that issue in one of several ways: by staying home on Sundays, coming late, bringing toys, or removing them from the nave when they've become disruptive. Fr. Paul from St. George's Cathedral in Rossport, Ohio, says the problem with these approaches is that they do nothing to connect the child with worship. They only serve to pacify the child and make others happy because they don't hear the noise. "When I hear the 'holy noise' of children in church," he says, "it makes me very happy because it tells me the parish has a future. We should be worried when we no longer hear that noise."

What you want to do, then, is to figure out how to help connect the child with what is happening. Don't depend solely on osmosis for that. Some helpful guidelines might include:

1. Do not expect children to sit still and act like adults. Ignore the raised eyebrows and disapproving frowns of the older ladies who've forgotten what it was like when their children were young. But do bring the child's attention to certain parts of the Liturgy, such as the Gospel reading and the Entrances. Expect them to stand at certain times. Even a two-year-old will then understand that something important is happening, even if he is not sure what that something is.

2. Bring them to church on a regular basis and be there at the beginning of the service.

3. Sit or stand in front—there is nothing more boring than looking at people's backs.

4. Feel free to move quietly around, letting the child touch and kiss icons.

5. Discuss some of the things that happen during the Liturgy *before* coming to church, but in a way that expresses joy in being fortunate enough to experience worship. That means you have to understand the Liturgy yourself. (A good, simple-to-read book to help you is *Let Us Attend*, published by Ancient Faith Publishing.)

6. If you want to bring something to occupy their attention, be sure that it is church-related. There are a number of excellent, beautifully illustrated picture books available now for Orthodox children—or make a little "church book" of your own. Orthodox coloring books are available also. Some parishes have Divine Liturgy books for children in the front pews. Toys are not appropriate, especially those that make loud clunks when dropped.

7. It is all right to take a disruptive child out and walk around a bit on rare occasions and as a last resort. Just keep in mind that your goal is to connect them with the worship, so allow a reasonable amount of that "holy noise" before removing them from the nave. Don't allow this to become a manipulative action on their part.

8. Establishing positive behavior patterns at home will go a long way in dealing with behavior issues at church. Handling a disruptive child during the Liturgy will be easier if the expectations—and the consequences of failing to meet those expectations—are clear at the outset.

All of the above suggestions are just tools, means to an end. They may not even be the best ways to get to where you want to go. The real goal is for you to help your child realize the heart of the Liturgy: God gives us the gift of Himself in Holy Communion.

In fact, there is a marvelous exchange of gifts connected with the Eucharist that impresses children once they are made aware of it. First, God has given us the gifts of wheat and grapes. People make bread and wine from these gifts, and then they bring them to the church to offer them back to God. But the exchange of gifts is not finished yet, and that is the best part: the Holy Spirit changes our gifts of bread and wine to the Body and Blood of Jesus.

When we receive Holy Communion, we receive the greatest gift of all: God Himself. We are joined to Him in a very special way. We cannot explain it; it is a mystery. We just know that it happens. Because we are so thankful for this gift, we want to offer God a gift in return, the gift of worship. We want to make up our minds to abide in Christ. When I am discussing communion, I focus on these points. The children learn the consecration prayers and know that the prayer to the Father to send down the Holy Spirit upon us and our gifts (the epiclesis) is a key moment in the Liturgy.

Orthodox worship is a major area where we are different from other Christian groups. Many people are convinced that the rituals of Orthodoxy are wrong and lead to apathy and the vain repetition condemned by Scripture, yet just the opposite actually happens. When we worship in the Orthodox liturgical way with our heart really in it, our worship becomes deeper. We are touched inwardly in a way that does not happen otherwise.

ACTIVITIES

1. **Discover the Connection (ages 6 and up)**
   Go outdoors and look for vines. Notice how each branch is connected to the stem. Read John 15:5 after you come indoors.

2. **Role Play Parts of the Liturgy (ages 3 and up)**
   Various parts of the Liturgy involve movement and lend themselves well to acting out. These include the Entrances, the Gospel reading, the anaphora (or offering), the consecration, the epiclesis, and receiving communion. Be sure to discuss the appropriate behavior for each.

3. **Bake the Prosphora**
   Help your children bake the bread used for communion. If you have never done this before, it is best to have an experienced baker help you the first time. One year in my parish, a small group of Sunday school

students got together during Great Lent and baked all the loaves that were used in the Pascha service.[33]

4. Discuss the Church's Invitation to Communion (ages 9 and up)

Begin the discussion by asking, "If you knew you were going to meet a king on earth, how would you prepare for the meeting, and how would you behave?"

In communion we are meeting the King. The Church invites us to this awesome meeting with the words, "With the fear of God, love and faith draw near!" What does this mean? What is the Church asking of us?

This is an invitation to three spiritual states:

1. *Fear* fills us with the desire to prove worthy of such a majestic, awesome, loving Lord and King. It is not a fear that is inspired by lack of trust in the Lord's ability to save us, but rather one that humbles us with awe.

2. *Love* is the desire to give our entire hearts to the One who is Love (1 John 4:8).

3. *Faith* is believing and confessing that Jesus is "truly the Christ, the Son of the Living God, who came into the world to save sinners, of whom I am the first."

As long as the children are interested, continue the discussion about approaching communion with our hearts right with God.

---

33 For more information about the prosphora and a recipe, see: http://gocportland.org/prosphora.html/

CHAPTER SEVEN

Journey to Bethlehem

*He who defines all things and is limited by none is contained in a
small, makeshift manger. He who holds the universe and grasps it in
the hollow of His hand is wrapped in the narrow, swaddling bands
and fastened with ordinary clothes. He who possesses the riches for
inexhaustible treasures submits Himself voluntarily to such great
poverty that He does not even have a place at the inn; and so He
enters a cave at the time of His birth, who was brought forth by God
timelessly and impossibly and without beginning. And—how great
a wonder! (St. Gregory Palamas)*

*Behold, the virgin shall conceive and bear a Son, and shall call His
name Immanuel. (Is. 7:14)*[34]

By the time you finish this chapter you should realize that:

⨭ God's love for us becomes apparent as we reflect on the
Incarnation.

⨭ It is possible to follow a well-lit sacred path precisely
because Christ became man for us.

And you should be motivated to:

⨭ Help your child reflect on the mystery of the Incarnation
and to know the events surrounding Christ's Birth.

---

34 *Immanuel* is translated "God with us."

FOLLOW THE PATH

Many years ago I was attending Liturgy on the Feast of the Annunciation to Mary. March 25 fell on a weekday that year, so as usual, only
a handful of worshippers were present. To be honest, not even quite a
handful—more like four, including the priest and the chanter.

After the service, the priest lamented, "If only our people understood what it means that God became man for us, this feast day would
be as important to them as Pascha. The church would be full." I nod-
ded in agreement, yet I must confess, I didn't realize how profound
that statement was until quite recently.

I did notice, though, that when my Greek Orthodox parish celebrated March 25 each year on the Sunday closest to that day, it was
only a commemoration of Greek Independence Day. No mention was
ever made of the Annunciation. In reality, March 25 was chosen to
celebrate Greece's liberation from Turkish rule *specifically* because at the
Annunciation our delivery from the oppression of sin was announced,
and Jesus, as man, began growing in Mary's womb. The people who
set that date recognized the significance of the day and its connection
to their struggles.

Christ is the Way, the Truth, and the Life of the world. The path
to communion and union with Him is well lit. This becomes increasingly apparent when we contemplate Christ becoming man at a specific point in time, at a specific location in the world, all because of
love—the love of the Divine Creator for His creation.

The Incarnation is central to Orthodox doctrine; we declare it as
truth in every Liturgy when we say in the Creed, "Who for us men and
for our salvation came down from heaven, and was incarnate of the

Holy Spirit and the Virgin Mary, and became man." In Jesus, God took on flesh and became man. This event fulfilled God's promise to Abraham; it completed the Law of Moses and fulfilled the Old Testament prophecies concerning the coming of the Messiah.

Many Church Fathers taught that even if Adam and Eve had not sinned, God still would have become man because He loved us so much. They say the Fall made the Incarnation an act of salvation as well as an act of love. Jesus, by becoming True God and True Man, has reopened the path for all humanity to unite with God. This is the basis for our liturgical hymn "Only Begotten Son." Our joyous response to God's voluntary act is proclaimed in the Troparion for the Annunciation:

> Today is the beginning of our salvation,
> The revelation of the eternal mystery.
> The Son of God becomes the Son of the Virgin
> As Gabriel announces the coming of Grace.
> Together with him, let us cry to the Theotokos:
> "Rejoice, O Full of Grace, the Lord is with you!"

The Feast of the Annunciation has such an important place in Orthodox theology that the rubrics decree the Liturgy of St. John Chrysostom is always celebrated on March 25 even if it falls on Pascha or Holy Friday. (In actuality, this coincidence is not possible in those Orthodox churches following the new calendar, but it can happen with old calendar churches and in the Churches of Finland and Estonia.)

The Gospels remind us frequently of the humanity of Christ as well as His divinity. Even those lengthy genealogies in Matthew and

Luke show us a man like one of us. They present a family background of sinners and saints—ancestors who had shortcomings, faults, and struggles, just as we do. This is what makes God accessible to us. Someone has said, Christ came to us just as we are. He came down so that we might be lifted up. He brings us up from humanity's filth and stench of decay to an everlasting relationship with Him.

For my younger Sunday school students, I present the story of the Annunciation (from Luke 1:26–38) during Advent because I want it to be easy for them to make the connection to Christmas. I would consider choosing a time closer to March 25 for the older ones. The materials I use for the presentation include an angel and a Virgin Mary from a Nativity set and "Mary's house," which is a small wooden box without a lid that I purchased in a craft store. I turn this box on its side so the open part is the front of the box—like looking into a dollhouse with no front wall. The house is not necessary. The story can be told without it, or with a simple backdrop made from lightweight cardboard cut and folded into a triptych shape.

I might also discuss the icon of the Annunciation with the children, pointing out the position of the angel's feet. It looks like Gabriel is running to share the news with Mary. His hand is extended toward Mary as he announces the marvelous blessing bestowed upon her. The Virgin sits on a throne, a place of great honor. She holds a spindle of yarn, depicting a tradition that says she was preparing fabric to be used for the veil in the temple when Gabriel appeared to her.

If the Lord God went to such great lengths to bring Himself to us, to light our path, why do we keep behaving as though we are walking in darkness? We don't have to. St. Maximos once said, "The Divine Logos, who once for all was born in the flesh, always in His compassion desires to be born in spirit in those who desire Him. He becomes an infant and molds Himself in them through the virtues. . . . The great mystery of the Incarnation remains a mystery eternally."[35]

St. Gregory Palamas said, "Prior to the Incarnation of the Logos of God, the Kingdom of Heaven was as far from us as the sky is from the earth, but when the King of Heaven came to dwell among us and chose to unite Himself to us, the Kingdom of Heaven drew near to all of us."[36]

SEEING THE GREAT LIGHT

I still remember an "aha" moment during my Montessori training. My Christian instructor was presenting a timeline of the history of human-kind (one of the materials we present in the Montessori classroom). After she unrolled the long vinyl timeline on the floor, she began placing miniature objects at the appropriate years. *The first object she placed was a miniature baby Jesus in a manger-crib* on the line dividing the BC and AD years. I got it right away, before a word was spoken. Christ is the center of everything that has ever happened in the past, everything that happens now, and everything that will happen in the future! All history is, in reality, our own personal salvation history.

Most of us Orthodox Christians in America have gotten our Christmas celebrations all backwards, succumbing to the influences of the West. Instead of remembering that the Nativity fast (or the forty days before Christmas) should be a time of repentance and

---

35   St. Maximos, *Philokalia Vol. 2*, Kallistos Ware, G. E. H. Palmer, Phillip Sherard, trans. (Faber & Faber, 1995), pp. 166–167

36   St. Gregory Palamas, *Philokalia Vol. 4*, Kallistos Ware, G. E. H. Palmer, Phillip Sherard, trans. (Faber & Faber, 1995), pp. 372–373

reflection, a preparation for the great feast, we get involved in parties, gift exchanges, and the un-Christian commercialism of the season. Sometimes it may be a Christian act to do the gift exchanging—say, for example, with co-workers at a pre-Christmas dinner—as it might seem standoffish or uncaring to refuse to do so. In some circumstances it is better to respect the practices of others than to hold to the letter of the law. However, in our interactions with Orthodox brothers and sisters, we should observe the rule: no parties and no breaking the fast until after receiving Holy Communion on Christmas Day. A truly Orthodox observance would be to continue during the days after December 25 with joyous festivities.[37]

Two nice customs that originated in Western Christianity but are fitting for Orthodox families are the Advent wreath and the Jesse Tree. Both are a great way to teach children about the true meaning of Christmas, and you can find information about both by searching online.

The Advent wreath is a circular arrangement of evergreen branches representing eternity. In that wreath we set candles, one for each week of the Nativity fast (of the liturgical color your parish uses for Advent) and one white "Christ" candle in the center. (Or all the candles can be placed in the wreath, with the candle for Christmas being a different color.) Each week we light one candle while meditating on one aspect of our spiritual preparation for the coming of the light of Christ into the world. We light the Christ candle on Christmas Eve or Christmas Day.

The Jesse Tree depicts the family tree or genealogy of Christ. It

---

37   Many excellent ideas for this can be found in *Celebrating the Twelve Days of Christmas* by AmandaEve Wigglesworth (Conciliar Press, 2012).

tells the story of our salvation history—God's great plan for us, beginning with creation, continuing through the Old Testament, to the coming of the Messiah. You can make a small tree from a tree branch firmly stuck in a pot. Each day of the Nativity fast (or each of the 25 days in December), hang an ornament on the tree representing either a prophecy of the Messiah or an ancestor of Christ. On Christmas Day, add a Jesus ornament. The name "Jesse Tree" comes from Isaiah's prophecy: "There shall come forth a Rod from the stem of Jesse, / And a Branch shall grow out of his roots" (Is. 11:1).[38]

These practices—fasting, preparing ourselves spiritually, activities that teach the Bible—help impress upon our souls and our children's souls the true meaning of Christmas. And what is that?

The first Christians did not celebrate the Birth of Christ. About AD 200, St. Clement of Alexandria mentions a commemoration in Egypt on May 20. In the first part of the fourth century, the Birth of Jesus, the adoration of the wise men and shepherds, and the Theophany or Baptism of our Lord were all celebrated together as one great feast marking the coming of Christ into the world. We Orthodox still, liturgically speaking, consider the days from Christmas to Theophany as one continuous day of celebration.

One of the reasons the Church decided in the fourth century to separate the commemoration of the Nativity of Jesus from that of His Baptism was to combat a prevailing heresy. The followers of Arius denied that Jesus was of the same substance as God; they taught that He was only the highest of created beings. (This false teaching has become popular again today.) According to this erroneous belief,

---

38 You can find directions for an Orthodox Jesse tree at http://festalcelebrations. wordpress.com/2007/12/27/jesse-tree-project-2008/

Christians could not celebrate the birth in flesh of God Himself, but only the birth of a very special creature who was not in reality God. By separating the feasts, the Church hoped to make clear the truth about the Incarnation.

Several theories exist as to why December 25 was chosen as the date for celebrating Christ's Birth. One theory proposes that the Church Fathers borrowed the symbolism of the sun from a pagan festival held at the time of the Winter Solstice. They thought to elevate or transform the pagan feast to a Christian understanding of the "Sun of Righteousness," the "Light of the World," etc. It's a popular theory, but probably wrong, say other researchers, who point out that it only began circulating around the twelfth century.

While the early Church certainly felt compelled to draw Christians away from pagan practices, the simplest explanation for choosing the December 25 date might be the most plausible: it was nine months after March 25, the date already set to celebrate the Annunciation, when Christ was conceived in Mary's womb.

Interesting debate aside, the real significance of Christmas is this: We don't commemorate simply the birth of a great man or an inspired prophet or an elevated master, but the coming of our Lord and Savior; God coming down so that we might be lifted up; the arrival of the second Adam, who conquered the death the first Adam brought into the world; the most awesome Love that willed to establish a relationship between Creator and creature. The Christmas message is as much about Christ's victory over death and His gift of eternal life as is the message of Pascha.

If there is one point to impress upon the child, it is this: Christmas is the coming of the Light into the world. From the darkness of sin and its consequences we can move, through Jesus, into the illumination He provides. He offers us the light we need to know (see) God.

> Not in glory and magnificence, but in poverty, wretchedness and humiliation does the Creator and Lord of heaven and earth appear in the world; not a luxurious palace, but a humble cave, receives the King of those who reign and the Lord of those who rule. By this we are shown the greatness of humility, poverty, meekness and simplicity, and the ruinousness of pride, riches, vainglory and luxury. . . . By this it is suggested to us that the Lord receives all and everyone: He is pleased by unlettered simplicity, when it is united to faithful fulfillment of one's calling, to purity of conscience and life; and He does not reject human wisdom when it knows how to submit itself to illumination from above and make use of its learning for the glory of God and the benefit of one's fellow men.[39]

ACTIVITIES

1. **Sculpey Clay Figures (all ages—with the adult making for younger children and older children making their own)**
   Sculpey clay is a product you can find in craft stores. It is available in white and various colors. Sculpey becomes pliable as you knead and work with it. While this polymer clay is flexible enough to be pulled without breaking, you can form shapes that will harden permanently after baking. Use it to make Bible characters and other small objects to use in the retelling of Bible stories.

   To save on the amount of clay used (and to cut down on the baking time), I wad up some foil into a cone shape about three to four inches high. This forms a base for the body. I flatten the top slightly, then

---

39   *Orthodox Word*, Vol. 3, 1967, pp. 16–17

for the head I stick a small ball of foil onto the body with a toothpick. Mold the Sculpey clay around the foil base about 1/4-inch thick and bake at 275 degrees for 15 minutes.

You can use white clay, then sand and paint after baking, or you can use the colored clays and make everything on the figure the color you want to begin with. You can blend the clays to create new colors. Hints: Don't make arms stick out. They will break off too easily. And don't try to add a lot of details; the fewer the better, and easier for you.

Keep the items for each story organized on trays or in baskets, placing them neatly on your sacred shelf.

You can also find recipes for inexpensive, homemade play doughs that will harden when baked or air-dried. They will be less durable, however.

2. Christ is Born!

Have a Nativity set on your sacred shelf that children can use to retell the story of the Birth of Christ. Buy or make individual figures that children can move around. You can make Sculpey clay figures. Unpainted wooden people and angel-shaped figures can also be purchased from several sources (see website listings on page 149 or do an online search under wood craft supplies/peg people).

Since our Christmas hymns speak of Christ being born in a cave, you might want to make a papier-maché cave. Papier-maché can be purchased at craft stores, but you can make your own with newspaper and homemade flour-and-water paste. To make a cave, first form the shape by wadding up aluminum foil. When it is the size and shape you want, you are ready to apply the papier-maché. Beware! It is messy, so you will need to have a protective covering over the table.

Prepare flour-and-water paste in a fairly large bowl. Start with one cup of flour. Mix in water gradually until the paste is a thick but slightly runny consistency. Tear newspaper into strips. Dip the strips into the paste and start applying to the cave base, overlapping as you go. Apply several layers, making sure the base is covered thoroughly. You may need to make more paste if the original batch was not enough. Let the cave dry. This may take several days. The thicker the paste, the shorter the drying time will be. When dry the cave can be painted.

CHAPTER EIGHT

Journey to Pascha

Pascha, the feast of feasts, is when heaven bows down to our poor earth and transfigures everyone and everything with its unwaning light. This is why Pascha was, is, and will be for every Orthodox soul the real spiritual, ultimate and only goal of its whole life. It is the longed-for goal of being eternally with the Risen Savior after the general resurrection of the whole human race.

However, we often forget that the way to this eternally blessed Pascha passes inevitably through the Holy Week of the Passion.[40]

By the time you finish this chapter you should realize that:
- Preparing for Pascha with the "bright sadness" of Lent helps us to enter into the joy of Pascha more fully.
- Family participation in the Holy Week and Pascha services makes a long-lasting, powerful impact upon a child. "Pascha was, is, and will be for every Orthodox soul the real spiritual, ultimate and only goal of its whole life."

And you should be motivated to:
- Help your family grow in understanding Pascha and nurture the desire to participate as much as possible in as many of the Holy Week services as you can.

---

40 From an Easter homily by Metropolitan Vitaly, 1998

KEEP YOUR EYES ON HIM

My husband and I good-naturedly joke that if we ever got a divorce, it would be because of all the arguments we've had on trips. When traveling, I'm supposed to be the navigator. He's supposed to follow my directions. Neither of us is always very good at our self-assigned roles. We get lost easily. I tease him about once getting lost in a tiny town that has only one main street running through it (the street that doubles as a state highway). You can't blink or you miss the town. We didn't really get lost, but when the road turned, Ivan kept going straight and we ended up in front of someone's house on a side street. If we had not turned around and gotten back to the main highway, we would never have reached our destination.

Spiritually speaking, we need to keep on our sacred path by heeding the proper directions. We have to pay attention to where we are going or we can easily get lost. Our destination becomes obscure. We have difficulty reaching it. Fortunately, when it comes to our spiritual journey, if we do lose our way, God in His great mercy is willing to get us back on the right track. He has marked our way with clear road signs that are spelled out by the Church. But we need to interpret those signs correctly. Ivan read a sign that said, "Road turns ahead." He thought mistakenly that he had to turn off the road, when in fact it meant that he should stay with the road as it turned.

One of the road signs for Orthodox Christians is Great Lent. As Alexander Schmemann says:

> When a man leaves on a journey, he must know where he is going. Thus with Lent. Above all, Lent is a spiritual journey and its destination is Easter, "the Feast of Feasts." It is the preparation for the

"fulfillment of Pascha, the true Revelation." We must begin, therefore by trying to understand this connection between Lent and Easter, for it reveals something very essential, very crucial about our Christian faith and life.[41]

One thing about us Orthodox Christians: We never jump suddenly into anything. Throughout our liturgical year, we're frequently getting ready, or preparing, for something. In the case of Pascha, we not only spend time preparing for the Feast of all Feasts, we prepare ourselves for preparing. On each of the five Sundays before Lent, the Church draws our attention to various aspects of repentance through the Gospel readings.

For example, on the Sunday of Zacchaeus we hear the story of a man who desired to see Jesus but was too short to see him in a crowd. We are reminded, as we hear how he climbed up into a tree in order to fulfill his desire, that *our* desire has to be in the right place. If we have no real desire to approach Christ, how can we expect Christ to respond to us as He did to Zacchaeus? (See Luke 19:1–10.)

And so it is for each successive week: we are invited to get our hearts ready for the real activity of Great Lent. "Let us stress once more that the purpose of Lent is not to force on us a few formal obligations, but to 'soften' our heart so that it may open itself to the realities of the spirit, to experience the hidden 'thirst and hunger' for communion with God."[42] All this preparation might seem unnecessary to some, but just thinking about how much time it takes for my heart to soften makes me suspect that the Church is very wise in its

---

41   Alexander Schmemann, *Great Lent: Journey to Pascha* (Crestwood, NY: SVS Press, 1969), p. 11
42   Schememann, *op. cit.*, p. 31

analysis of human nature, and consequentially, in its guidelines for Lent.

When my children were small, family life was simpler than it is now. We were not always frantically trying to juggle schedules for one organized activity or event after another. My boys got themselves to sports practices, school, or visits with friends. I seldom had to be a taxi driver for my family, yet I would have had difficulty making it to all the Lenten services, reading all the Bible passages, or following all the Lenten practices. I can imagine that it might be even harder for families now. But everyone can resolve to do something. Choosing one Presanctified Liturgy to attend, for example, is an attainable goal for anyone whose job does not conflict with service times. If it's not, we should rethink our priorities.

If the focus of Great Lent is repentance and softening the heart in preparation for receiving the Light, how do we undertake this monumental task with children? Especially since it is so difficult for us? When we ourselves are so full of pride that we see no serious need of repentance?

Perhaps with the very youngest there is little need to do anything, but as the children grow physically and in moral awareness, they should also grow in the understanding of Lent's spiritual significance. Introduce them to fasting. Arrange a time for the whole family to go to confession. Decide on a Lenten project. Do something to let the children know this is a special time to get ready for Pascha. Read stories about saints who illustrate good examples of ways people can change their lives. Read some of the Bible passages from Genesis that are designated for Lent. Involve older children in a discussion of Isaiah 53:4–6. Who bore our sins? Who suffered for us? Who was led like a lamb to the slaughter? Meditating on these things stirs up our hearts, making repentance easier.

And what is repentance to begin with? If we confuse this word, *metanoia* in Greek, with mere remorse or feeling sorry for something we've done wrong, we are mistaken. Metanoia is a fundamental transformation or change of mind. When we repent, we determine to turn away from our sinful condition that has caused us to lose sight of our destination and once again get back on the right track. Someone has said that repentance is not a self-contained act; it is a passing over, a Pascha from death to life, a continual renewal of that life. I would add that it is reconciliation—reconciliation of a soul that has strayed off the path with the True Light, who guides us faithfully.

Repentance leads to (but is not the same as) confession. Our confession with a priest as our witness before God is the result of repentance, not the cause of it. Confession is a closure of sorts, a means of convincing our spirits that we are done with this sin. That we should get over it, let it go, knowing that God in His loving mercy has forgiven and forgotten it. Furthermore, He is not just now getting around to forgiving our particular wrongdoing. He forgave all sin on the Cross, but it remains up to us to access His forgiveness, as He does not enter the door of our heart without an invitation.

Confession fills us with divine grace, which frees us from burdensome guilt feelings. Yes, we can make confession directly to God—and should do so the moment we realize we have sinned. But confession to God as both priest and penitent stand in front of the icon of Christ is part of the healing process of our diseased soul. The guidance we receive from our spiritual Father is often clearly inspired by the Holy

Spirit. It helps us in becoming more like God. Confession is never viewed as a legalistic rite. It is a healing balm.

COME, RECEIVE THE LIGHT:
CHRIST'S VICTORY OVER DEATH

Connall's father brought him regularly to the Liturgy and other services. When Connall's mother was not able to attend, another woman of the parish sat with Connall in the front pew while his father served at the altar. Even when he was very young, Connall noticed the action around him and was drawn to the various movements. At one service during Holy Week, his father became apprehensive when he discovered his faithful helper was absent. The service was going to begin in a few moments. What was he going to do with Connall? Connall was then under three years old.

The woman's advice on the phone must have created even more apprehension: She couldn't be there because she had to work, but assured Connall's father, "Just sit him down in the front pew. He'll be all right."

And Connall was fine, although there was one touching incident. The small boy was so fascinated by everything going on that he wanted to get a closer look. He went up to the solea and stretched out on his belly, chin resting on his palms, elbows on the floor, to watch. One parishioner tried to pick Connall up and take him back to the pew. I don't think the church has ever heard louder screams! The man left him there, albeit a little closer to the edge of the solea where he wouldn't get stepped on. That's where Connell spent the rest of the service, happy, content, and quiet. Years later, Connall was a first-grader in my Sunday school class when he exclaimed during a discussion, "Pascha is my favorite!"

While participation in the Paschal services is of supreme importance, some preparation and explanation beforehand is advisable. A highlight of our Sunday school year that the students never get tired of repeating is our Paschal celebration. After weeks of preparation, we have a special ceremony—in essence a role-playing of what they will see and hear at the Resurrection Vigil.

Since I have been doing this celebration with the youth of our parish, I have noticed a gradual change in their attitude toward the Vigil itself. Children have always liked the part about lighting and holding the candles, but they also used to complain about the length of everything that came afterward. It was boring, they said. Many fell asleep. A large number of parents didn't even bring their children.

Last year nearly all my students attended the Paschal Liturgy and were awake, looking alert the entire time. When I invited them to share their feelings about their experience, I got responses like, "I loved it!" When I asked them if the service was too long or boring, they all said, "No!" They had been prepared. They had worshipped the risen Lord. They understood that this was a celebration of Christ's victory over the darkness of death.

Having beheld the Resurrection of Christ, let us worship the Holy Lord Jesus, who alone is without sin. We venerate Your cross, O Christ, and we praise and glorify Your Holy Resurrection. For You are our God, and we know no other except You, and we call on Your Name. Come all you faithful, let us worship Christ's Holy Resurrection; for through the Cross, joy has come to the whole world. For at all times, blessing the Lord, we praise His Resurrection. Having endured the Cross for us,. He destroyed death by death. Having risen from the grave, as He foretold, He has given us eternal life and great mercy. (Prayer from the Paschal service)

In order to understand the symbolism of Pascha, you have to understand the Jewish festival of Passover. When the Israelites were slaves in Egypt, Moses was chosen by God to lead them out of that land, but Pharaoh would not listen to the Lord's servant. Because of the hardness of Pharaoh's heart, God sent ten plagues upon Egypt. The last one was the death of the firstborn son of every family. The Israelites would be spared from this plague, however. They were instructed to smear the blood of a spring lamb above their doorposts; by this the Lord would know to pass over those homes. While the Egyptians were mourning, the Israelites were able to flee and cross the Red Sea as if it were dry land, thus achieving freedom.

So significant is Passover that it is referred to time and time again in both the Old and New Testaments, even in our church hymns. For us, Christ has become our Passover. Instead of the Old Covenant animal sacrifices for the atonement of sin, He became the Paschal lamb who was willingly led to the slaughter. For the Jews, Passover celebrates God's steadfast love and freedom. It is the same for us as we celebrate His saving grace. Through the sacrifice on the Cross and His Resurrection, we experience liberation from sin, death, and evil. We receive a new life in a new land—the Kingdom of God.

Indeed, if it were not for the many typological details of the Passover and the exodus from Egypt, one might wonder why Christians would consider it more than an interesting, somewhat unpleasant story—one that could be ignored with ease. Some of the "types" in the Exodus 11–12 account include:

1. The blood of the male lamb that was smeared over the door-posts in the sign of the cross foreshadowed Christ's shedding of blood on the Cross.

2. The lamb had to be perfect, "without blemish." Christ was perfect.

3. The Hebrews passed through the waters of the Red Sea. We pass through the waters of baptism, going from the slavery of sin to walk in the newness of life.

4. The celebration of the Passover festival foreshadows the Eucharist.

At Pascha we sing the baptismal hymn: "As many of you as have been baptized into Christ have put on Christ. Alleluia." Why? What does our baptism have to do with this? I have already mentioned that in earlier centuries baptism was connected with Pascha. I would like to add here my paraphrase of some thoughts from a certain priest. It is because of Pascha that the bond with death has been broken—that we can truly live, truly be alive, and be in Christ. If we have not "put on Christ," there will be no resurrection to eternal life awaiting us.

ACTIVITIES

1. **Learn the hymn "Christ is Risen," or one of the other Paschal hymns.**
   Make a booklet containing the hymn and an illustration.

2. **Decorate Paschal candles to hold during the Resurrection Vigil.**

Purchase a candle for each family member. Candles should be large enough to last longer than the Vigil service, but small enough to hold with ease. Using acrylic paints and small brushes, paint crosses or simple designs on the candles. After you bring them home, put them in your icon corner or on the dining room table. Light them during prayers or at dinner on each Sunday during the Paschal season.

3. Attend as many of the Holy Week services as possible, always explaining to your children beforehand the significance of each service.

$\mathcal{D}$iscovering Pentecost

And it shall come to pass afterward
That I will pour out My Spirit on all flesh (Joel 2:28).

When the Day of Pentecost had fully come, they were all with one accord in one place. And suddenly there came a sound from heaven, as of a rushing mighty wind, and it filled the whole house where they were sitting. Then there appeared to them divided tongues, as of fire, and one sat upon each of them. And they were all filled with the Holy Spirit and began to speak with other tongues, as the Spirit gave them utterance (Acts 2:1–4).

By the time you finish this chapter you should realize that:
- Pentecost is the day the Holy Spirit came to us in His fullness.
- The same Holy Spirit who filled the apostles with God's presence and power can fill us with the gift of His presence and power also.

And you should be motivated to:
- Help your child realize that God can be real in our lives; that the Holy Spirit helps us know God.

BASK IN HIS GRACE

When I was younger I was involved for a time in the charismatic movement. For me it was an essential part of my spiritual journey. Before those days, the Holy Spirit (in my mind) was simply a person who was mentioned at the end of "in the name of the Father, and of the Son . . ." Because of the movement's emphasis on the Holy Spirit, I committed myself to investigating the role of the third person of the Godhead in Orthodox theology and practice. That was a real eye-opener!

Now I can rightfully ask myself, "In what aspect of Orthodoxy does the Holy Spirit *not* hold great significance?" I can think of none. Our liturgical and sacramental life breathes the Holy Spirit. We have a depth of theological understanding that charismatics do not have; Orthodox avoid the excessive emotionalism and mere surface understanding of spirituality that usually characterize the movement. Most of us begin our daily prayers addressing the Holy Spirit with "Heavenly King, Comforter and Spirit of Truth . . ."

A charismatic friend once attended an Orthodox baptism with me. She said afterward, "The Holy Spirit was really working here." Ours is truly a pentecostal church—with a genuine understanding of what the word *pentecostal* actually means.

Whatever the reasons God had for leading me on this detour, the end result was this: The Holy Spirit seems more real to me now. I have a deeper commitment to God. I have a greater love of our Faith because I can see how much more balanced it is than what I witnessed in that past experience.

Orthodoxy teaches that the Holy Spirit does guide the individual, but always within the framework of the Church. That is not to say the

Holy Spirit will only be active in us when we are in church; but if we are not partaking of the Eucharist, confessing our sins, praying and fasting, listening to His Word and the counsel of our spiritual father, we will lack the discernment to discover God's will or know which entity is truly at the source of our experience. We will be more easily tempted to go off in the wrong direction. We also know that God will only intervene in our lives in an unusual way when it is a spiritual necessity and is according to His will, not ours.

If we consider three of the greatest feasts of the Church, we can say this: Christmas marks the time the Father gave us the gift of His Son; Pascha the triumph over the power of sin; and Pentecost the granting of the gift of the Holy Spirit. Through the sacraments and the Word of God, the Holy Spirit gives us the faith to believe in Christ and work toward our personal theosis.

Perfecting our faith, growing in holiness, requires certain interior qualities or virtues. These are the gifts we receive in the sacrament of chrismation. God gives them to us freely out of unconditional love, not based on any worthiness we might want to claim—but they can remain inactive and uncharged if we don't make a deliberate choice to plug into them, if we don't keep using them. Our Helper, the Holy Spirit, is the source of the power we need in our Christian struggle.

Without Pentecost, the Church would never have grown. Without experiencing a personal Pentecost in chrismation, you and I would have no hope of fulfilling God's intentions for us. We need to understand what happened at Pentecost and what happens to us because of Pentecost.

The Gospel reading for the day is Acts 2:1–11. Here in this short passage, we learn of an event that fulfilled the first part of Joel's prophecy, turned the world upside down, changed the course of history, and birthed the Church. It was an event that caused the startled witnesses to accuse the Apostles of drunkenness, not realizing they were intoxicated with the power of the Holy Spirit, not with wine.

The Jewish Pentecost (also called the Festival of Weeks or Festival of the First Fruits) commemorated the giving of the Ten Commandments to Moses on Mt. Sinai fifty days after the Exodus. It was a harvest festival at which the Jews offered the first fruits of their fields to God. After Jesus' ascension into heaven, the Apostles and others, including Mary, gathered together in an upper room as they had been instructed by our Lord. They were to wait for the coming of the Holy Spirit, which happened on Pentecost.

On the day of the festival, crowds of people from many nations gathered to celebrate Pentecost. The Gospel gives a dramatic account of the miracle, describing a roaring sound like wind, flames of fire, and speaking in tongues. The Apostles, with an unprecedented boldness, began preaching about Jesus. They were on fire with enthusiasm. The miracle was that each person heard the Apostles' words in their own language—those extraordinary words spoken boldly by ordinary men. The Apostles received the fullness of the Holy Spirit, His power, so they might spread the gospel beyond the tiny realm of the Jews. Instead of the first fruits of the harvest, the Apostles were the first fruits of the Church. They needed all the power and courage and help they could get.

The first time I did a presentation on Pentecost and the gifts of the Holy Spirit to a group of children, I thought they'd never get it. But I plunged into the lesson, and the reception was enthusiastic. In fact, the next year when I did the same lesson, one child smiled broadly and exclaimed, "Oh, I remember this!" He sat up straight in eager anticipation of participating once again.

The Bible contains several lists of gifts of the Holy Spirit. These lists are not all the same. In the New Testament, specific gifts, such as teaching, mercy, or prophecy, are named. These generally are gifts needed for specific ministries. No one person will receive all of these gifts—only the ones he will need for his specific role in the Body of Christ, or to handle a specific, temporary situation. And no one person decides which gift He will get. "The breath of the Holy Spirit falls where it will." I do not introduce these gifts to the children, but rather the seven found in Isaiah 11:1–2 (wisdom, understanding, counsel, might, knowledge, godliness, fear of God)—gifts we all need in order to live fruitfully in God's Kingdom.

Wisdom is penetration into divine truth. It detaches us from the world and makes us desire only the things of God. The better we understand God's truth, the more we value it. Through wisdom we are able to contemplate God and have a proper perspective on the world, which is His creation. Wisdom, the desire to know God, is the most important of the seven gifts. Without desire everything else dissolves into uselessness. The definition I give to children is, "The gift of wisdom helps us want to know all the things of God and love all of them."

Understanding is different from wisdom. While wisdom gives us the desire, understanding enables us to know. We become certain of the truths of God. Understanding rises above natural reason, which is concerned only with things we can explain in the world around us. Thus, we can be certain of the doctrine of the Trinity even though we cannot explain it in the same way as we can a mathematical equation. In the language of the young child, it could be defined as "knowing our faith very well."

Counsel builds on wisdom and understanding, allowing us to judge rightly what we should do in a particular circumstance. This gift manifests itself in us as a heaven-sent intuition. It allows us to make prompt decisions with little or no thought. The counsel of the Holy Spirit assures us we will act correctly in times of tribulation. Through His counsel the Apostles spoke boldly and truthfully about the Faith at Pentecost. They did not have to think about what they were going to say beforehand. The words just came forth, directed by the Holy Spirit. In the language of the child, counsel is "the gift that helps us always do what is right."

Might (or fortitude) is also sometimes called *courage*. It is the gift of strength given when we are required to stand up for what is right. It is not rashness or foolhardiness, but the quiet inner power that helps us overcome our fears and remain steady in the face of obstacles. The saints and martyrs exhibited the gift of fortitude in extraordinary ways. In the language of the child, this is "the gift that gives us the strength of God."

Knowledge allows us to see the circumstances of our lives as God sees them, though in a limited way. Through exercising the gift of knowledge, we discern God's purpose in our lives and His reason for placing us in our particular circumstances. This gift has been referred to as "the science of the saints." As this gift is perfected in us, we can more easily distinguish between the promptings of God and the temptations of the devil. The saints have often manifested this gift to a high degree. The explanation for the young child can be as simple as, "it helps us learn more about God."

Godliness (or *piety* or *holiness*) is an instinctual response to the faith perfected in us through the gifts of wisdom and knowledge. Through the gift of piety we are compelled to render to God worship and service, not out of a sense of duty or with a feeling of drudgery, but as an act of love. Our giving glory to God becomes a natural response of communicating with someone we love and desire to honor. In the language of the young child: "This is the gift of loving God the Father and Jesus, our Good Shepherd."

Fear of God (*reverence, awe of God*) does not mean being afraid of Him. The type of fear the Bible mentions most frequently is a reverential awe of the Lord's majesty. However, it also demands a proper respect for the wrath and anger of God. Awe of God implies an acknowledgement of all that God is—a dispenser of justice as well as our loving Shepherd. Approaching the Eucharist with the fear of God means that when we come to partake of His Holy Mysteries, humbled with awe, loving Him, and full of thankfulness for the Gift we are receiving, we have only to fear falling into sin and failure to repent. Fear of God bubbles up inside of us quite naturally as we grow spiritually. The child can be told, "This gift is respect and reverence for God."

Perhaps one of the reasons so many young people drift away from the Church when they reach college age is that they do not comprehend Pentecost. Perhaps they have not realized on a personal level that God keeps His promises; that the Holy Spirit is more than a name we mention when making the sign of the cross; that Jesus sent the Holy Spirit to pour out His gifts upon all who desire to become like God. Keep Pentecost and the action of the Holy Spirit in mind as you go about the business of raising godly children.

GETTING PAST DETOURS, ROADBLOCKS,
AND WRONG TURNS

So far I've made it sound like following the sacred path with your children is a snap, haven't I? All you have to do is follow a few guidelines, live a godly life yourself, involve your family in church life, spend time creating and doing some activities together—and lo, there you are—saints with offspring who are all saints.

Oh, I wish it were that easy! A little thing called struggle is bound to come along. You'll meet obstacles. You'll find that it's hard work raising godly children, and some days you'll feel as if you are a complete failure. Things won't always go the way you want. A child might rebel, or decide he no longer wants to go to church, or become involved in drugs. Domestic violence or mental illness might be an issue. Chronic or serious illness can create physical and emotional strain. You will make mistakes along the way as you deal with each particular circumstance, but that is where our Orthodox faith offers us solace and advice.

Struggles have a purpose in our lives. I once read on Facebook (original source unknown), "Problems are like washing machines. They twist us, spin us, and knock us around—but in the end we come out cleaner, brighter, and better than before." Our Orthodox Faith does not offer us a "feel good always" life of ease, but rather the assurance that God stands with us through everything that threatens to slam us to the ground.

Perhaps the biggest challenge Orthodox parents face today is maintaining an Orthodox ethos in the family while living in a non-Orthodox culture, one which is often in stark opposition to our beliefs.

This is an attractive world, and we, as well as our children, are often drawn into it in subtle ways we don't even realize. We are called to live in this world; the danger comes when we forget that we are to be lights reflecting the glory of God rather than a part of the world's waywardness.

God has never promised us an easy path. Quite the opposite: He says the way is narrow and difficult. If there is one saint in the history of the Church who escaped temptation, times of mental anguish, difficulties in living God's way, or tribulation of some kind, I don't know his or her story.

I can remember many years ago a Christian woman, Corrie Ten Boom, wrote a book about her experiences in a Nazi prison camp. The conditions were so bad in her barracks that the guards refused to step inside. The building was infested with cockroaches and lice, for one thing. Corrie told her sister they were to give thanks for these bugs that were creating much misery for the prisoners. Later they realized it was precisely *because* of the absence of the guards that they were free to pray and read a smuggled-in Bible. The bugs were a blessing from God.

"In everything give thanks," the Bible says. It also commands, "Rejoice in the Lord always. Again I say rejoice." When you have grown as a Christian, you begin to realize that difficulties and trials are the very things that increase the Holy Spirit in us when we respond in God's way. They are the gifts that perfect and strengthen us. We are what we are, not *in spite* of what we have gone through, but *because* of it. When you truly comprehend this in your spirit, you can give thanks always and mean it.

Each day brings an obstacle for a parent to overcome. And each small victory bears spiritual fruit. Setbacks in reaching goals will happen. Consider them opportunities to learn, to take inventory, perhaps to repent and restructure. Know that episodes of struggle are only temporary detours or wrong turns unless we allow them to become permanent roadblocks.

When you face an obstacle (which can be defined as any distraction or situation that prevents you from achieving your goals), you are at a crossroad; you will have to choose how you will respond—God's way or another way. Following God's way may not seem smoother, but it will always get you to your eternal destination; other ways will not.

Whether you're confronting obstacles or basking undisturbed in God's love during a blessed moment, the Holy Spirit is within you to be your Comforter, your Spirit of Truth, Treasury of all Blessings, and Giver of Life. His gifts will be operating, helping you according to your specific need.

Remember also that when you are in the midst of a difficulty, you may not have the energy, the will, or the time to take complex measures to rectify the situation. It's best to keep your responsive action simple. During trying times, and this may include (as far as your soul's spiritual condition is concerned) apathy and lack of commitment to the spiritual welfare of your family, there are steps you can take to access God's help. In taking them, we discover who we really are, and we become aware of His faithfulness.

Remember who is in control. *Surrender* yourself completely to God. Don't try to manipulate Him into doing your will. Trust in His purpose even when you don't understand it. Choose to believe He will carry you through anything and everything. Pray, "Give what is needed, O Lord. Your will be done." Or simply say, "Lord, have mercy."

Lean on Christ and His Word. There have been moments in my life when the only thing I could do was repeat a brief scripture over and over. Those moments, in retrospect, led to intense encounters with God—not as intense as what the saints have experienced, but all that I could handle at the time, enough to keep me going. There are so many scriptures suitable for this remedy that I hesitate to single out just one. The Holy Spirit will direct His counsel and help toward the immediate need of an individual.

The person leaning on a specific scripture might need a psalm verse that praises the Lord or offers encouragement, or helps her remember His blessings. Sometimes you come across a scripture in the Bible or while reading a book that seems to leap out at you and capture your attention. That is the one God wants to impress upon your inner being. It is the one that serves your special need. If this does not happen with you, or if you have previously been unfamiliar with the Bible, you may find a verse that calls to you in the next chapter. Sometimes another person you encounter will say just the right words you need to hear at the exact moment you need to hear them. Often they will not even know why they spoke them.

It is said that prayer moves mountains. Sometimes a parent may feel it would be easier to move a mountain than to struggle with a difficult or rebellious child. On good days and bad days, you must *pray diligently*. "Men ought always to pray and not lose heart" (Luke 18:1). Prayer on the good days will hold you through the challenging ones and direct your path. When in distress, you will find hope. "Prayer is a great weapon, a rich treasure, a wealth that is never exhausted, an undisturbed refuge, a cause of tranquility, the root of a multitude of blessings and their source" (St. John Chrysostom).

Prayer is always the first line of defense in tribulation or indecision. In 2 Chronicles 20, Jehoshaphat, king of Judah, is being threatened by enemies of the kingdom. What does he do? He calls the nation together for prayer. As a result, the Holy Spirit, through a prophet, tells Jehoshaphat what to do: show up for battle, and God will win the victory. Our task is to show up for the battle by taking whatever step(s) God expects of us. He will do the rest.

Also, you must *arm yourself for battle.* By that I mean spiritual warfare. Books have been written about it. The saints and fathers talk about who we are really fighting in our spiritual struggles, but it seems to be a topic the average lay person knows little about. Ours is a constant battle with the forces of evil. The demons tempt us, and all too often, we fall simply because we do not recognize the wiles of the devil. Ephesians 6:14–18 describes the armor of God—the armor that protects us from the assaults of evil.

> Stand therefore, having girded your waist with truth, having put on the breastplate of righteousness, and having shod your feet with the preparation of the gospel of peace; above all taking the shield of faith with which you will be able to quench all the fiery darts of the wicked one. And take the helmet of salvation, and the sword of the Spirit, which is the word of God; praying always with all prayer and supplication in the Spirit, being watchful to this end with all perseverance and supplication for all the saints.

Do you know what this means? The gifts of the Holy Spirit we received at our baptism and chrismation provide us with the weapons we need to become triumphant Christians. Nurturing these gifts in your children will take you and them a long way in your spiritual journey.

What is the spiritual battle? Well, the soul is a garden divided into two parts. On one hand are planted thorny bushes, and on the other half, flowers. We also have a water pump with two taps and two channels. The one guides the water to the thorns and the other to the flowers. I always have the choice to open one or the other tap. I leave the thorns without water and they dry up. I water the flowers and they blossom.[43]

ACTIVITIES

1. Celebrate the Birthday of the Church (any age)

Bake a cake and put twelve candles on it to represent the Twelve Apostles. Read and discuss Acts 2.1–11. Point out that on this day the Holy Spirit gave the Apostles the power to spread the good news of Jesus to people all over the world.

2. Role Play "The Seal of the Holy Spirit" in Chrismation (ages 3 and up)

You will need a small container of olive oil (add some perfume for fragrance), Q-tips, and a card that reads, "The seal of the Holy Spirit." Demonstrate how the person being chrismated is anointed. Dip the Q-tip in the oil and anoint the following body parts of the child or a doll (repeating the words "the seal of the gift of the Holy Spirit" with each anointing): forehead, chest, eyes, ears, lips, hands, and feet. Explain that this helps us serve God with all our strength and body and soul. Discuss how we might serve God with our mind, our heart, our hands and feet, etc. How can the seal of the gift of the Holy Spirit help us to walk in the way of God's commandments?

---

43 Elder Porphyrios, from *Precious Vessels of the Holy Spirit* (Protecting Veil Press, 2003), p. 170

CHAPTER TEN

𝒜 Lamp to Guide the Way

But now your children will utter songs and dances of Satan, like cooks, and caterers, and musicians; no one knows any psalm but it seems a thing to be ashamed of, even a mockery and a joke. There is the treasury house of all these evils. For whatsoever soil the plant stands in, such is the fruit it bears; if in a sandy soil, of like nature is its fruit; if in a sweet and rich one, it is again similar. So the matter of instruction is a sort of a fountain. Teach him to sing those psalms which are so full of love of wisdom. When in these you have led him on from childhood, little by little you will lead him forward even to the higher things. (St. John Chrysostom, Homily IX on Colossians)

By the time you finish this chapter you should realize that:
- Children need frequent exposure to Scripture, beginning at a very early age.
- The Word of God is a treasure, and neglect of it causes harm.

And you should be motivated to:
- Introduce your child to the Bible in small pieces at a time.

LET IT SHINE

A group of religious educators had an interesting discussion. Should you read Bible stories to young children from a storybook, a beginner's Bible, or the Scripture itself? Good arguments were given for each approach, but most of the participants felt that preschoolers were too young to be introduced to Scripture directly from Scripture. When a catechist said she reads to her young group right from the Bible, very few understood how that could work.

When Leo Tolstoy observed that his students were most receptive to religious instruction when he read from the Bible and gave them time to reflect on the meaning of its words, he was talking about older students. Will word-for-word reading directly from Scripture hold the attention of the younger ones? Will it nurture their understanding and knowledge? Will it help them to fall in love with God?

Of course not if you start reading at a spot such as 1 Chronicles. The first nine chapters of this Old Testament book contain nothing but genealogies, and it is certainly not recommended as a starting point even for an adult beginning reader. You have to introduce the Bible little by little in ways that are at the level of the child. This may begin by letting them see *you* reading Scripture when they are infants. Board books containing single Bible stories are available for toddlers, and you can find an increasing number of Orthodox picture books, as well as two Orthodox Beginner Bibles.

A most effective, informal way of making the Bible come alive is to raise readers in the home. Story time, aside from its entertainment purpose, has other less obvious ripple effects. Story time is bonding time between the adult and child—an encounter with love. It can nurture curiosity and motivate the desire to read. You can use story time to show God's love and to spark a desire to become more familiar with what God says.

In my Sunday school classroom we have an Orthodox Study Bible on a stand (actually a plant stand I brought from home). When the Scripture source for the lesson is very short, as is the parable of the mustard seed, I will have a bookmark at that place and read directly from it. I will turn the Bible around and point to the words. "Look, this is where it says . . ." Even the three-year-olds will stretch their necks to see. Every child wants to get a good look. Give your children their own Bible that they can keep in a prominent place (on their icon stand, on a special shelf, etc.). Even if they don't read it, they will develop a reverence for Scripture. At the very least, provide them with a beginner Bible book.

What is the Bible and what place should we give it in the Ortho-dox home? St. John of Damascus called it "a scented garden, delightful and beautiful." St. John Chrysostom claimed the devil does not dare to enter where the Gospel lies. He said also, "It is not possible . . . ever to exhaust the mind of the Scriptures. It is a well which has no bottom." He warned, "Let them hear, as many of us as neglect the reading of the Scriptures, to what harm we are subjecting ourselves, to what poverty." Others have called the Bible the sacred book of the Church, a treasure, a medicine chest with remedies for grief and troubles. People have accurately described the Bible in many ways.

The Bible contains a history, but it is not like any other history text we have ever read. It has a beginning and an end, a theme and a goal, and a thread running through it tying all the loose ends together. The story Holy Scripture tells is yours and mine; it is the history of our salvation and that of every human being who has lived or ever will live on this earth—sacred history. Above all, the Bible is a revelation, or rather, the written account of that revelation. God has revealed Himself to us. He is involved in our history. He came into the world incarnate as Jesus Christ. And through Jesus we are involved in the life of God. That's the Bible's message.

Orthodox Christians, however, as much as we reverence the Bible, do not approach it as isolated individuals attempting to put our own interpretations on the words we read. We do not bend its genuine message to the foolishness of our personal thoughts, which have likely been tainted by our culture and ignorance. We come to the Bible as members of the Church. We note how Scripture is used in our worship and how it was interpreted by the Holy Fathers. We adhere to the scriptural declarations of the Creed. Our approach is to keep the message of the Bible pure and unadulterated through the living Tradition of the Church. It is a liturgical and patristic outlook.

The true meaning of the word *tradition* refers to the revelation made by God and delivered to us by the Apostles. Tradition with a big "T" is more than a tradition with a little "t" or something that is handed down from one generation to another. The Tradition of the Church is the living, dynamic breath of the Holy Spirit at work—yesterday, today, and tomorrow.

Can you think of one worship service of the Orthodox Church that does not have Bible readings? No, because there is none. Even the words of the services themselves are largely drawn from Scripture. Holy Scripture, worship, and theology are tightly intertwined in the Orthodox mind; we cannot separate them into distinct, separate categories. If you are going to raise godly children in an Orthodox home,

you will need to help them fall in love with God by introducing them
to the Bible (if only by discussing the Gospel reading on the way to
or from Church), by involving them in church life, and by teaching
them what we believe. You can't leave out any one aspect, or place one
above another.

Many Orthodox adults have grown up biblically challenged. This
is not a criticism; it's just the way it is. If you are one of these, the next
few paragraphs are for you.

The Bible is not one book, but a collection of books, written by
many different authors over a span of centuries. All the books now
included in these sacred writings were determined by the early Church
to be divinely inspired, revealing the essentials of our salvation history. It is a book of the Church for those who belong to God's chosen
assembly of believers—a book designed to assist us in our spiritual
journey by revealing the relationship God desires to have with us.

The Bible is divided into two main sections: the Old Testament
and the New Testament. There are forty-nine books in the Orthodox Old Testament and thirty-nine in Protestant versions. The New
Testament contains twenty-seven books. The content matter of the
Old Testament is referred to as the revelation of the Old Covenant,
and the New Testament describes our New Covenant relationship
with God.

The Old Testament shows how God prepared the world for the
coming of Christ. It speaks of Creation, the Fall, and the role of His
chosen people, the Jews, in our salvation history. It records how God
made covenants (or agreements) with them, promising to be their God
if they would be His people by obeying Him. In the Old Testament
we learn that time after time, the Jews (or Hebrews) broke their end of

the agreement. They kept disobeying, repenting, returning, and then disobeying again in continuous cycles.

Modern-day critics make accusations that the Old Testament God is harsh, judgmental, and wrathful—a God that seems unlikable. Yet I look at the Old Testament stories and see beautiful glimpses of God's love, mercy, majesty, and faithfulness when the people were obedient. I see a God not willing to give up on them—or us. I see the desire of the Old Testament heroes to worship the Almighty and seek after Him even in adverse conditions. I see men like David, who committed terrible sins such as murder and adultery, repent and find forgiveness, providing assurance that God can and will forgive anything if only we turn to Him.

The New Testament proclaims that Christ the Messiah has come to bring us into a new relationship with Him. The New Testament is the fulfillment of everything God promised in the Old. This section of the Bible includes four Gospel books, one history of the beginning of the Church, twenty-one epistles (or letters), and one book of prophecy. The New Testament reveals that God has established the means of our salvation through Christ. Whereas God once demanded animal sacrifices and burnt offerings from the Jews to atone for their sins, it is now Christ who is our atonement. It is He who is the Paschal Lamb. And it is He who will bring us to the throne of grace in heaven.

Yet if we think of the Bible, particularly the Old Testament, as simply history, we miss its significance and depth. Scripture contains several levels of meaning: the literal or historical account, the spiritual or allegorical meaning, and the personal message for the individual reader. For example, in Genesis we read the story of the creation of Adam and his expulsion from the Garden of Eden because of his sin.

That is the literal account. This, however, points to a higher truth revealed in the New Testament: Just as Adam brought sin into the world, so Christ destroyed the power of sin, freeing us from its bondage. The story of Adam foreshadows the story of Christ. One cannot truly understand the Old Testament without some knowledge of its typology.

And what is the personal message we are to discern when reading about Adam? I'll leave that to you to discover.

As far as introducing our children to Scripture is concerned, our most important goal is to instill in them a sense of the joy waiting to be unveiled in God's Word—how it can transport us into the realm of the divine, a life with God. This can be accomplished by reading Bible stories, pointing out how the Liturgy is biblically based, meditating on Bible passages with them, memorizing verses, and doing Bible-related activities. The child should become more familiar with the people of God than with the superheroes of television and movies.

As far as where an adult should start if tackling the Bible for the first time, I'd say with the Psalms or one of the Gospels. See the Ancient Faith Publishing catalog or website for a list of available commentaries. You can also purchase an *Orthodox Study Bible* from them.

GATEWAY TO A CHILD'S HEART

The five senses are the gateway to the preschooler's heart. In order for anything to have lasting value and meaning at this age, the senses must be involved. Activity is essential.

As an adult, can you look back on something you learned or became interested in *because* of something an adult had you *do*? For me, it was a sixth-grade teacher who taught us about the Roman Empire by dividing the class into small groups and letting each group choose a hands-on project related to that activity; we were then to present our project to the class. Even earlier than that, a Sunday school teacher had us act out a Bible story.

Activities don't have to be complex or require great artistic capabilities. The finished product does not have to shout "talent." As a matter of fact, preschoolers are more satisfied with the process than with the end result of their endeavors. They don't really care how it looks; they just love that they did it.

As an example of what I'm talking about, let's say you want the family to memorize a Bible verse. A somewhat effective, but possibly short-lasting method is this: During one sitting, have everyone recite the verse numerous times until they can say it without a prompt. A better method is to print the verse on cardstock and have the child make a decorative border. Keep the verse on the dinner table and have everyone say the verse together once a day, without worrying about how many days or weeks it takes to learn. This way they've listened, touched, and looked. God is entering into their heart through the senses.

Something else has happened. You've taught by permitting repetition, and you've presented the concept in small chunks. How much discussion and explanation will take place, or what you will emphasize about the meaning, will depend on the age of the child. If you are perceptive you can follow the lead of the child. Certainly if they start asking questions, they are interested. If they don't, it might mean they just need time to mull the concept over in their minds. Or they might be indicating "that's enough for now," or that they don't have the slightest interest because it doesn't meet a personal need at the moment.

Remember St. John Chrysostom's quotation at the beginning of this chapter? That's how I'm going to close this book. "When in these things you have led him on from childhood, little by little you will lead him forward even to higher things." Lock this reminder in your heart and examine it every now and then.

ACTIVITIES

1. **Mysteriously Appearing Words (ages 5 and up)**
    Cover a letter-sized sheet of white paper with wax paper. Pressing hard with a sharp pencil, write the verse on the wax paper. Make the letters large enough so the verse takes up a lot of space. Remove the wax paper. (Alternatively, write the verse in white crayon.) Have the child paint the white paper with watercolor. If you have pressed hard enough, the paint will not adhere to the wax and the verse will mysteriously appear.

2. **Make a Booklet of Memory Verses (ages 4 and up)**
    The Bible contains many beautiful verses to choose from. I've listed a few possibilities below. If your children are very young, feel free to shorten or paraphrase them. Use only one verse per booklet. I have used the New King James version, but you may find other translations you like better.[44] The Psalms have many beautiful verses to choose from. Children may wish to illustrate their booklets.

    > Oh, taste and see that the LORD *is* good;
    > Blessed *is* the man *who* trusts in Him! (Ps. 34:8)

---

44 Many Bible translations are available fully searchable at www.biblegateway.com.

The LORD *is* my shepherd;
I shall not want.
He makes me to lie down in green pastures;
He leads me beside the still waters. (Ps. 23:1–2)

Fear not, for I *am* with you;
Be not dismayed, for I *am* your God.
I will strengthen you,
Yes, I will help you,
I will uphold you with My righteous right hand. (Is. 41:10)

If we confess our sins, He is faithful and just to forgive us
our sins and to cleanse us from all unrighteousness.
(1 John 1:9)

Watch, stand fast in the faith, be brave, be strong. Let all
that you *do* be done with love. (1 Cor. 16:13–14)

I am the light of the world. He who follows Me shall not
walk in darkness, but have the light of life. (John 8:12)

But seek first the kingdom of God and His righteousness,
and all these things shall be added to you. (Matt. 6:33)

See also: Matthew 22:37–40; Psalm 1:1; James 4:10; Psalm 119:12;
Matthew 6:24; Luke 6:31; John 11:25; 1 John 3:11; Revelation 3:20;
Leviticus 19:18; John 14:6; Ephesians 4:8; 1 Corinthians 6:11;
Titus 3:5; Matthew 26:26–28; Romans 12:3

3. **Play a Hide-and-Seek Game (ages 3–8)**
Write verses on index cards and hide them around the room. Read the
verses when the child has found them.

4. Bible Verses in Calligraphy

Purchase a calligraphy pen at an art supply store or use a regular pen. Older boys and girls can write their favorite Bible verses on especially nice paper. (Simple calligraphy styles can be found on the internet.) Choose a verse to meditate on and memorize. Older children might enjoy designing a Bible verse card on the computer. Read the verse once a day until everyone knows it by heart.

Observing the Twelve Great Feasts in the Home

Great Feasts of the Fixed Cycle

BIRTH OF THE THEOTOKOS, SEPTEMBER 8/21[45]

God chose a dwelling place on earth (a tabernacle) to make His first preparation for mankind's salvation; this tabernacle had to be a spiritually pure vessel in order to hold Divinity. Mary was chosen to hold the Son of God within her womb. The righteous Anna and Joachim were her parents. According to tradition, Anna and Joachim were old and childless. Barrenness was a sign of God's disfavor among the Jews, but God answered their earnest prayers and Mary was born. Because of her holiness she would become the "house of God" and the "gate of heaven" that would unite God with men. This feast, like all the liturgical celebrations of the Theotokos, proclaims that we receive God's mercy because she bore our Savior. Through the Theotokos we can rejoice in our own salvation. With the birth of the Theotokos the transition from the Old Covenant to the New Covenant begins.

1. **Read or sing the Apolytikion of the Feast.**

    Your birth, O Theotokos, brought joy to the whole world,
    for from you dawned the Sun of righteousness, Christ our God.

---

45 The first date given for each fixed feast is the new (Gregorian) calendar date; the second is the old (Julian) calendar date.

> Freeing us from the curse, He gave us all His blessings.
> Abolishing death, He grants us eternal life.

This is one of the Vespers hymns for the feast. Explain that Mary is like a ladder that joins people here on earth to heaven and God.

2. **Tell the story of the birth of the Mother of God.**
   Use an icon of the event to help you.

3. **Bring blue flowers to the church.**
   Bring them as an offering to the Theotokos (blue is the liturgical color worn by priests on Mary's feast days).

ELEVATION OF THE LIFE-GIVING CROSS, SEPTEMBER 14/27

When we lift up the cross and bow down before it, we proclaim that we belong to God's heavenly Kingdom, not to this earthly one. Our eternal citizenship is in the city of God, where we are joined by angels and surrounded by saints. On this feast we rededicate ourselves to the One who died on the Cross, taking hope in His words from the Gospel of John, "And I, if I am lifted up from the earth, will draw all peoples to Myself" (John 12:32).

The Elevation of the Cross commemorates the finding of Christ's Cross by St. Helena in the fourth century. The practice of "elevating" the cross began in the seventh century, after the True Cross had been taken by the Persians and then recovered by the Emperor Heraclius. At first the feast celebrated the triumph over the political enemies of the Christian empire. Now we rejoice because, through Christ, our spiritual enemies are defeated.

1. Plant some basil in a pot (or outdoors if your weather permits) as a reminder of the basil that grew near the cross St. Helena discovered.

   Paint a cross on a rock and place it beside the basil.

2. **Sing or say the Hymn of Veneration.**

   Before the Cross, we bow down in worship, O Master,
   and Your holy resurrection we glorify.

THE ENTRANCE OF THE THEOTOKOS INTO THE TEMPLE, NOVEMBER 21/DECEMBER 4

Although this event is not found in the Bible but in the apocryphal Protoevangelion of James, it has great spiritual significance for Christians. The Theotokos entered the temple to become herself the living temple of God. It is through Mary that the old prophecies concerning Christ will be fulfilled. God will come to dwell with man and save him. And just as Mary, a human person, became a dwelling place for the Divine Presence, we too become tabernacles of the Lord ("Do you not know that your body is the temple of the Holy Spirit?" 1 Cor. 6:19). The entry of Mary into the temple marks the close of the Old Covenant era of our salvation history.

1. **Sing or read the Kontakion of the Feast.**

   Today the most pure temple of the Savior,
   the precious bridal chamber and Virgin,
   the sacred treasure of God,
   enters the house of the Lord,
   bringing the grace of the Divine Spirit.

The angels of God praise her.
She is the heavenly tabernacle.

2. **Create a blue vase and arrange some flowers to honor the Theotokos.**

    You will need several shades of blue tissue. Tear the tissue paper into pieces of varying sizes and shapes. Working in sections, brush generous amounts of Elmer's glue onto a glass jar (pint or quart size depending on how big you want it) with a paintbrush. Cover each section as you go with the pieces of tissue paper until no glass is showing. Be sure to overlap the pieces. Finally, cover the entire jar with another layer of glue. The tissue paper will get somewhat wet and some pieces might slide around a bit—no problem. Let the glue dry, and you will have a blue vase with a gloss finish.

3. **Make a temple from a shoebox.**

    Turn a shoebox onto one of its long sides. This side becomes the floor of the temple. The open area is the door. Make two cylinders from white construction paper or cardstock for the pillars. Glue a pillar on each side of the shoebox at the front. Paint the temple white or gold. If you like, make figures or use clothespin or peg dolls for the people in this event.

THE NATIVITY OF CHRIST, DECEMBER 25/JANUARY 7

On this day, the King of Majesty, who sits on a heavenly throne full of glory, comes down to lie in a manger. The wonder fills us with astonishment. Light has dawned for us, obscuring the darkness, bringing hope, promising the gift of reconciliation and transformation. The hymns of this feast are joyful, reflecting the joy in our hearts.

We celebrate, as we should. But let us not forget, in our celebrating, those who are suffering, alone, or homeless. Christ came to salve our wounds. Let us make the effort to be the healing balm for others who feel they have no cause for joy at Christmas.

1. **Give a gift to the poor.**

   Decide on something you can do for others. In our parish, several dedicated people prepare meals for the homeless once a week. At Christmas our Sunday school children create Christmas cards to give to these people. Each child designs a card. I scan the designs and print out enough cards so that each homeless person we feed at a special Christmas dinner will receive one. I ask the children not to write greetings on their design because they will invariably write something that might increase sadness in a homeless person. "Have a great Christmas" would only serve as a reminder that this Christmas is not so great for them. The message I put on the inside of the card will be something more encouraging such as, "We are keeping you in our prayers."

   Local charitable agencies often conduct special collection drives at Christmas. Choose one to donate to as your gift. Make it something that your children can participate in.

2. **Invite someone who would otherwise be alone to your family's Christmas dinner.**

   It could be a neighbor or someone from your parish.

THEOPHANY, JANUARY 6/13

Theophany (or Epiphany) means "shining forth" or "manifestation." On this day we commemorate the Baptism of Jesus and the revelation to the world that Jesus is the divine Son of God, One of the Holy

Trinity with the Father and the Holy Spirit. On Theophany we are reminded once again that God is with us.[46]

1. **Have your children prepare containers for holy water to take to Liturgy the day of the feast.**

   Plastic or glass containers with lids should be washed thoroughly, then may be decorated on the outside. A cross or small Theophany icon may be attached with rubber cement.

   Tell your children how we use holy water: We can start our day off by drinking a little. We can sprinkle it in our rooms when we want to ask for God's special blessing and there is no priest present. We can use it to bless icons, gardens, homes, and almost anything you want blessed. Any time we feel a special need, we can drink holy water or ask the priest to bless us with holy water. Parents can bless their children with holy water before they leave the house.

2. **Invite your priest to bless your home during the month of January.**

   With parents' guidance, children should prepare their rooms for the blessing and select one personal possession to be blessed as well: a new icon for their room, a baseball glove for an avid player, etc.

3. **Hold a dress rehearsal in preparation for the priest's visit to bless your home.**

   Practice singing the troparion together and plan the route for the children to lead their priest from room to room carrying a lit candle.

----

46 · The following activities are from http://www.theologic.com/oflweb/feasts/01-06. htm (which itself is from a compilation by Father Stephen Belonick, Binghampton, NY).

THE MEETING OF THE LORD,
FEBRUARY 2/15

When Jesus was forty days old, He was taken to the temple in Jerusalem. According to Jewish law, it was the first time Mary could enter the temple after giving birth. At this visit she was to offer a young lamb or two doves as a sacrifice to God. Because they were poor, she and Joseph brought doves.

In the temple were two elderly people, Simeon and Anna the prophetess, who had been waiting for the coming of the Messiah. Simeon had prayed that he would not die until this happened. God granted his request, and he instantly recognized the baby he held in his arms was the promised One. His canticle is sung daily at Vespers. Anna also recognized the Lord. Her reaction was spontaneous; she, too, gave thanks. And that was not all. She, who never left the temple, went out and proclaimed the Christ to everyone she met. Orthodox Christians see this feast as a meeting of God and man. The festal icon shows Anna holding a scroll that reads, "This Child has established heaven and earth."

1. **Read Luke 2:22–39.**

    Help children to write a play. Who are the important people in this story? (Mary, Joseph, Simeon, Anna.) How does your play begin? Where are Mary and Joseph at first? Where do they go? What offerings to God do they take? Who do they meet at the temple? What does Simeon do and say? What does Anna do and say?

2. **Show and discuss pictures of your child's blessing on his or her first visit to the church.**

My Forty Day Blessing Book by Christina Kyriacou is beautifully written and available from Light and Life Publishing.

3. **Mary and Joseph brought a gift (the doves) to offer to God. Think of a special gift you can offer to God today (or this week).**

    It can be baking cookies for a neighbor, attending a church service you usually miss, saying an extra prayer before going to bed, promising to always tell the truth, or anything you think would be special.

ANNUNCIATION TO THE THEOTOKOS, MARCH 25/APRIL 7

"Behold, the maidservant of the Lord! Let it be to me according to your word" (Luke 1:38). Mary's willingness to carry out God's wish for her serves as a model for us. Are we obedient? Do we desire to serve Him above all things? Do we rejoice and magnify the Lord along with the Theotokos? Teach your children the significance of the Annunciation.

1. **Make Sculpey clay figures for the Archangel Gabriel and Mary.**

2. **Make a booklet for this story (Luke 1:26–38).**

3. **Make a house for Mary by turning a shoebox on one side. Paint it.**

TRANSFIGURATION, AUGUST 6/19

The Transfiguration of Christ took place during the Jewish Festival of Booths, which commemorated the dwelling of God with men. When Christ shone like the sun and His clothes became as white as light, the truth was revealed: Christ is God dwelling with man. We can now realize that our destiny and that of all creation is to be transformed and glorified by God Himself.

1. Give a simple definition of the word *transfiguration*.
   Talk about things that change or are transformed in nature: the seasons, animals, plants, and climate. Go outside on a nature walk. Look for examples of things that undergo change or transformation. If you can, collect a few items or take photographs; use them to make collages when you come back inside.[47]

2. Read or tell the account of the Transfiguration (Matthew 17:1–9).

3. Take grapes to church to be blessed at the Transfiguration liturgy. If it is the custom in your parish to take other harvest fruits and vegetables also, include those. Some parishes take these baskets to shut-ins after they are blessed.

---

47 Adapted from a lesson by Dr. Constance Tarasar. For this and more detailed instructions for excellent ways to observe the Transfiguration Feast, see: http://www.oca.org/the-hub/catechical-themes-transfiguration/the-feast-of-transfiguration (*sic*)

DORMITION OF THE THEOTOKOS, AUGUST 15/28

According to Orthodox teaching, Mary died as all people die, because of her mortal human nature, yet she was without personal sin. She was saved by Christ and raised up by God into heaven in the fullness of her spiritual and bodily existence. We commemorate this assumption after a two-week fast. We hear in the Gospel reading for the day that the blessed state Mary already participates in belongs to all who "hear the word of God and keep it."[48]

1. **Wear the color blue to the Liturgy.**

2. **Make flowers out of different shades of blue tissue paper to decorate your icon corner.**

3. **Bring flowers to be blessed at the Liturgy.**

4. **Place a special candle in the center of your dinner table.**
   Light it when you sing the troparion of the feast and say your mealtime prayers.

Great Feasts of the Paschal Cycle

PALM SUNDAY, SUNDAY BEFORE PASCHA

On Palm Sunday we behold our King, not simply as the One who rode into Jerusalem on a colt, but as the Word of God made flesh—the

---

48 The following activities are adapted from a blog by M. Emily. See: http://charmingthebirdsfromthetrees.blogspot.com/2010/07/dormition-for-little-ones.html

One who comes to us ceaselessly in power and glory. This great feast speaks of the heavenly Kingdom and our place in it—the kingdom that is a present reality as well as a future glory.

1. **Sing or read the Kontakion.**

    Sitting on Your throne in heaven, You are carried on a foal on earth, O Christ God. Accept the praise of the angels and songs of children who sing: Blessed is He who comes in the name of the Lord.

2. **Help make the palm crosses that are blessed and given to worshippers on Palm Sunday.**

PASCHA

Pascha is called the Feast of Feasts because it is the most significant celebration in the life of Orthodox Christians. On this day the Paschal message rings out loud and clear: Death is defeated. As a student of mine wrote on one of his drawings, "Christ is the winner." Even the chains of the grave could not hold our Savior captive. Through the Cross and the Resurrection, Christ's victory over the darkness of sin and death releases us from bondage to sin and death. Through faith we are offered restoration, transformation, and everlasting life. On this day our hearts sing louder than on any other day, "This is the day the Lord has made. Let us rejoice and be glad in it."

1. **Dye eggs on or before Holy Thursday.**

    Decorated eggs are blessed and distributed to the faithful at the end of the Resurrection liturgy. They remind us that Christ rose from the grave. In the Greek tradition the eggs are dyed red to symbolize the blood of Christ. In Slavic traditions they are decorated with colorful symbols. It is customary to crack the eggs together at the Paschal meal. When doing this, the first person says, "Christ is risen!" The second person responds, "Truly, He is risen!"

2. **Invite a neighbor, or someone from your parish who might otherwise be alone, to your Paschal dinner.**

3. **Learn the Paschal greeting in various languages.**
   This reminds us that Christ's offer of salvation extends to all people everywhere.

ASCENSION, FORTY DAYS AFTER PASCHA

1. **Make a mobile.**
   Cut a round or oval shape from blue poster board (about dinner plate size). Attach four 24-inch-long ribbons, evenly spaced around the edge. Glue on cotton balls to represent clouds, leaving some of the blue showing. Make a stand for a small icon print of the Ascension. Glue the print, which can now stand up, in the center of the clouds. Bring the ends of the ribbons together and tie to form a hanger for the mobile. Hang from the ceiling.

2. **Blow bubbles in the air.**

PENTECOST, FIFTY DAYS AFTER PASCHA

(See Chapter Nine)

Some Helpful Websites

(ACCESSIBLE AS OF 8/15/2013)

1. http://www.illuminationlearning.ning.com
2. http://www.festalcelebrations.wordpress.com/ (has directions for Jesse Tree)
3. http://www.gocportland.org/prosphora.html/ (has information and recipe for prosphora)
4. http://www.st-demetrios.org/PDFs/artoklasia.pdf (information and recipe for artoklasia)
5. http://www.churchyearforchildren.blogspot.com
6. http://www.orthodoxcatechesis.org
7. http://www.orthodoxcp.wikispaces.com
8. http://www.saintkassianipress.com
9. http://www.orthodoxabc.com
10. http://www.oca.org/the-hub/catechical-themes (sic)
11. http://www.etsy.com/shop/ClickityClack/ (has unpainted pegs that can be used for peg people)

Much of the content of this book reflects the philosophy and method of a program called the Catechesis of the Good Shepherd. Becoming a CGS catechist requires intensive training from an authorized trainer. Find information about the Catechesis at: http://www. cgsusa.org.

About the Author

Elizabeth White was chrismated in 1964 at Holy Trinity Greek Orthodox Church in Spokane, Washington. She has worked as a Montessori
teacher, an instructor for a Montessori teacher training course, a director of Spokane Montessori School, and the supervisor of her parish's
Sunday school program. Currently she is semi-retired, being involved
only part-time with her school. She is the author of several curriculum materials for the Department of Religious Education of the Greek
Orthodox Archdiocese of North America.

Also by the author

Walking in Wonder: Nurturing Orthodox Christian Virtues in Your Children
Blends patristic Orthodox teaching with practical suggestions for
parents, resulting in a book that is not only inspirational but full of
common sense. Elizabeth draws from her extensive experience as an
educator, parent, and faithful Orthodox Christian to outline not only
what the virtues are, but how their development can be encouraged in
the lives of children 8 and under.

Paperback, 72 pages, ISBN 978-1-888212-69-3

Available from store.ancientfaith.com

Ancient Faith Publishing hopes you have enjoyed and benefited from this book. The proceeds from the sales of our books only partially cover the costs of operating our nonprofit ministry—which includes both the work of **Ancient Faith Publishing** (formerly known as Conciliar Press) and the work of **Ancient Faith Radio.** Your financial support makes it possible to continue this ministry both in print and online. Donations are tax-deductible and can be made at www.ancientfaith.com.

Bringing you Orthodox Christian music, readings, prayers, teaching and podcasts 24 hours a day since 2004 at

www.ancientfaith.com